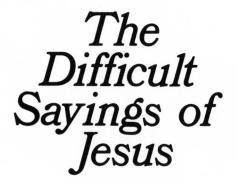

# The Difficult Sayings of Jesus

*by*
WILLIAM NEIL

WILLIAM B. EERDMANS PUBLISHING COMPANY
GRAND RAPIDS

*This American edition published by special arrangement with A. R. Mowbray & Co Limited, The Alden Press, Osney Mead, Oxford, England, who issue the book under the title* What Jesus Really Meant.

**Library of Congress Cataloging in Publication Data**
Neil, William, 1909-
    The difficult sayings of Jesus.
    1. Jesus Christ—Words. I. Title.
BT306.N4      232.9′54          75-14059
ISBN 0-8028-3467-1

# Contents

# A NOTE TO THE READER

We are happy to introduce to American readers these illuminating treatments by one of Scotland's best-known Bible teachers of some familiar but perplexing remarks of Jesus recorded in the four Gospels. The passages dealt with by Professor Neil have puzzled many devout Bible readers over the years. Moreover, critics of the Bible have seen in them an opportunity for discounting the truth and relevance of the gospel.

The problem Professor Neil addresses in these thirty-four short chapters arose before the words of Jesus were ever committed to writing. Even during his ministry, what Jesus said was often misunderstood by his hearers. The New English Bible renders with especial vividness the reaction of some of the disciples to what Jesus taught in the synagogue at Capernaum: "This is more than we can stomach! Why listen to such talk?" (John 6:60). A few verses later we learn the outcome: "From that time on, many of his disciples withdrew and no longer went about with him."

The saying of Jesus that occasioned this response (discussed in Chapter 32 below) was "I am the bread of life"—one of the beloved "I am" texts of the Fourth Gospel. How many throughout the history of the church have ever comprehended fully the blessing and promise of this claim is another question—as attested by the bitter controversies that have always surrounded the Eucharist.

Not every saying classified as "difficult" is perplexing for the same reasons. Sometimes Jesus' meaning seems clear enough . . . until one tries to apply what he said to a particular case. What does it mean to render to Caesar what is Caesar's and to God what is God's? How are we to live out Jesus' warning to Peter that all who take the sword die by it? When must we turn the other cheek?

Some difficult sayings trouble us with their moral rigor. Think of Jesus' standards for divorce. Or his instruction to the rich young ruler about selling everything and giving to the poor. Or his advice that one cut off an offending hand or pluck out a wayward eye. Does he not understand the weakness of the human nature he came to redeem?

Some statements sound callous, if not actually immoral. Think of his seemingly cruel response to a would-be follower who wanted first to bury his father and then to come with Jesus. Or his praise for the astuteness of worldly people—we would call them scoundrels—in dealing with their own kind. Or his threat that the one who has will be given more, and the one who has not will forfeit even what he has. Is this the Friend of the downtrodden and the dispossessed speaking?

For the person who thinks to fit Jesus neatly into a theological pigeonhole, some of the Master's words can be particularly difficult. Those who insist too strongly on the radical differences between Christianity and any other form of worshiping God will stumble over Jesus' statement that it is from the Jews that salvation comes. Yet Jesus also rebukes those who would return legalistically to Jewish religious practice. He tells us, for instance, that the Sabbath was made for man, not *vice versa,* a suggestion that surely aroused the wrath of his more orthodox listeners. Again, there are those who stress the name "Prince of Peace" for Jesus. But we have it on his own authority that he came to bring not peace but a sword.

These are but a few of the difficult texts which Professor Neil treats, clearly and directly. What shines forth here is not simply the lucid exposition of the background of the sayings, setting them in perspective and removing their difficulty. For Professor Neil, understanding Jesus' words is not a question of solving a puzzle to satisfy idle curiosity. As is evident on every page of this book, understanding the difficult sayings of Jesus is but the first step in a new appreciation for the challenge of Christian faith. In a real sense, when we understand the difficult sayings of Jesus, our difficulty has just begun.                    THE PUBLISHERS

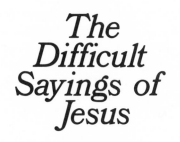

*The*
*Difficult*
*Sayings of*
*Jesus*

# 1

## RECONCILIATION NOT RETALIATION

*If someone slaps you on the right cheek,*
*turn and offer him your left. . . .*

*Love your enemies.*

JESUS' WORDS about "turning the other cheek" are often quoted derisively by opponents of Christianity as the supreme example of the futility and impracticality of Christ's teaching. What would have happened, they ask, if we had turned the other cheek to Hitler? And are we to stand by benevolently while a thug attacks our mother, only murmuring that our sister will be back shortly? Questions of this sort are obviously based on muddled thinking or wilful misunderstanding. There is, of course, some excuse for misunderstanding if we confine ourselves to the King James Version, "Resist not evil; but whosoever shall smite thee on thy right cheek, turn to him the other also." This certainly sounds like a demand by Jesus for nonresistance in cases of violent attack.

The New English Bible, however, makes it plain that this is not so. Jesus is contrasting the Old Testament principle of "an eye for an eye and a tooth for a tooth" (Exod. 21:23–25), the law of retaliation (Matt. 5:38), with the new principle by which his followers must be guided, the desire for reconciliation. "Do not set yourself against the man who wrongs you," he says in verse 39; that is, do not retaliate in cases of unfriendly attacks upon yourselves. But putting up with a slap on the face is obviously not the same as risking a blow with a blackjack from a burglar. In that case self-

3

defense would be common sense, and protection of helpless victims a Christian duty. A slap on the face is merely a picturesque way of describing a personal insult, and, in this event, turning the other cheek means refusing to return the insult but rather ignoring it. This saying has therefore nothing to do with arguments for or against pacifism, violence or nonviolence, or indeed political, military, or police action of any kind. Jesus is dealing purely with personal relationships.

And as so often in his teaching, he throws out a challenge by startling his listeners with the unexpected. They had become accustomed to his way of making people think by saying something amusing—"If someone gives you a clout on the side of the head. . ." (pause while they cudgel their brains as to what they were supposed to do; then comes the least likely answer) ". . . let him clout you on the other side as well!" We can see from the next few verses (Matt. 5:40–42) that Jesus does not mean his hearers to take him literally, for he goes on to talk of a man being sued in a law court for the recovery of his "shirt" (the long undergarment worn next to the skin, which together with the "coat" on top for cold weather formed the sum total of a man's clothing). If this happens, says Jesus, let your creditor have the coat as well—which would of course leave the man naked except for his loincloth!

The other two illustrations make it abundantly clear that Jesus' language is figurative. The first is that of a Roman legionary picking on a passerby and ordering him to carry some heavy load for a mile along the road, as Simon of Cyrene was compelled to carry Jesus' cross (Mark 14:21). If this happens to you, says Jesus, offer to carry it twice as far—the proverbial "second mile"—obviously the last thing a reluctant conscript would dream of doing. But it is the principle of responding to harshness with kindness that Jesus is commending. So with Jesus' last example. "Do not turn your back on a man who wants to borrow." To obey this literally would encourage spongers, and reward the shiftless and thriftless at the expense of those who work for their living. Jesus is obviously not commending indiscriminate charity, which is demoralizing, but rather urging us to cultivate the spirit of generosity. While this has strictly nothing to do with avoiding retaliation, it does show that the whole passage is not concerned with laying down laws for Christian behavior but with the attitude a Christian should adopt in dealing with people in general. Reconciliation and magnanimity must point the way.

Jesus crystallizes his teaching on this aspect of the Christian life in the memorable words: "Love your enemies" (Matt. 5:44). Like the saying about "turning the other cheek," this has proved a happy hunting ground for those who scoff at the remoteness of Christian teaching from everyday life. Let us once more see these words of Jesus in their proper context. He is still talking about personal relationships and not about nations at war or enemies of the state. More important, when he says "love" he does not mean "like." How could we possibly be asked to *like* someone who is bent on breaking up our home life, destroying our marriage, leading our children into bad habits, spreading malicious gossip about us, or making trouble for us in our jobs? Yet Jesus tells us we should *love* such people. What does he mean?

Clearly he does not expect his followers to love those who do them an injury in the same way as they love their wives and families, their parents, and their best friends. He urges us, however, to take as our example God, who sends the blessing of rain and sunshine on all alike, good and bad, honest and dishonest. We must show a like good will in our own circle to all and sundry, whether we like them or not, helping where our help is needed in the spirit of the Good Samaritan. St. Paul grasps the sense of our Lord's words when he says: "Do not let evil conquer you, but use good to defeat evil" (Rom. 12:21). Disregard of personal insults, forgiveness of wrongs done to us, generosity of spirit to friends and enemies alike—these are the marks of Christian discipleship.

# 2

## PEACE THROUGH STRIFE

*You must not think that I have come to bring peace
to the earth: I have not come to bring peace,
but a sword.*

Matthew 10:34

THE BIRTH OF CHRIST, which we celebrate at Christmas, is generally thought of as promising peace on earth (Luke 2:14); and in one of the great choruses of Handel's *Messiah* Christians have always understood the words of Isaiah 9:6 about the coming of the Prince of Peace to refer to Jesus. On the first Christmas of World War I, German and British troops in the front line spontaneously left off shelling each other and joined in singing Christmas carols and making gestures of good will, because they felt instinctively that war in all its horror was the utter denial of the spirit of the Christ whom both sides had been brought up to honor. Since then in time of war a Christmas truce, official or unofficial, has seemed to be the right way to recognize at least for this short period that peace and not war is what Christianity stands for. Did not Jesus say: "All who take the sword die by the sword" (Matt. 26:52)?

Yet here Jesus appears to be saying something quite different, namely that his mission was not to bring peace to the world but a sword, almost as if he were proclaiming a Holy War, as followers of Muhammad were to do several centuries later. And indeed, taken out of their context these words were used by fanatical Scottish Covenanters in the religious wars of the seventeenth century to justify their blasphemous war cry: "Jesus and no quarter!" If, however, we look at the words that follow verse 34 Jesus' meaning

6

becomes clear. Verses 35 and 36 continue the thought of verse 34: "I have come to set a man against his father, a daughter against her mother, a son's wife against her mother-in-law; and a man will find his enemies under his own roof." These words are adapted from Micah 7:6; and they make it plain that Jesus is not speaking of war at all, either of war between nations or of civil war within the same nation, but of conflict within the same family. St. Luke's version of the same saying (Luke 12:51) confirms this: "Do you suppose I came to establish peace on earth? No indeed, I have come to bring division."

We can see this happening in the story of the early church when within ordinary families one or two members would become converts to Christianity as a result of the evangelism of the missionaries. Other members of the family would choose to continue in their old faith—whether Jewish or pagan—and argument, discord, and bitterness would ensue. The harmony of the family was destroyed. But we do not need to look back to the ancient world. Any missionary in the young churches overseas today can tell story after story of the breaking up of families in India, Africa, and elsewhere when some have responded to the Christian gospel and others have preferred to continue in their old ways. The result is a divided house. It must require superhuman courage for a member of a Hindu or Moslem family to break with the traditions of centuries and face the contempt—indeed, hatred—of relatives who see conversion to Christianity as a betrayal and an unforgivable sin. Mahatma Gandhi, who had a deeper understanding of the Christian way than most nominal Christians in the Western world, could not bring himself to sever his connection finally with the Hindu background in which he had grown up.

There is, however, a wider sense in which Jesus' words in Matthew 10:34 may be taken. Having lived through two major wars in half a century and with the ever present shadow of possible annihilation darkening our future, most of us think of peace as the absence of armed conflict and in some moods can wish for nothing better for our children than that they should grow up in a world from which war and the fear of war has been banished forever. But as Studdert Kennedy said, "War is kinder than a Godless peace." There are some kinds of peace that are not worth having—peace at any price, peace that perpetuates injustice, peace that exists under tyranny. Europe and the world could have had peace under Hitler's Thousand Year Reich, with concentration camps and gas chambers for those who criticized the regime.

Christ certainly came to bring peace, as every page of the New Testament confirms. But he stood for real peace and not a bogus peace. His peace must be fought for; and that involves conflict and division, as his words in Matthew 10:34 remind us. As followers of Christ we are committed to fight against the evil in ourselves and in our society in the light of the guidance we have been given. It is a battle against greed and selfishness, against cruelty and oppression, against injustice and indifference, wherever they may be found. The gospel is a gospel of peace through strife, not peace through apathy or evasion of responsibility. Peace in the home, the office, the factory, and in society at large is not achieved by everyone agreeing with everyone else but by everyone standing up for what he believes to be true and right. Of course this will mean disagreement and discord, opposition, and often bitterness. But the peace that Christ came to bring can only be realized by striving to reconcile our differences in charity but with honesty, or, as St. Paul puts it, by speaking the truth in love (Eph. 4:15).

# 3

## THE POWER OF FAITH

*If you have faith no bigger even than a mustard-seed,*
*you will say to this mountain,*
*"Move from here to there!", and it will move;*
*nothing will prove impossible for you.*

Matthew 17:20

TWO ELDERLY SISTERS who had spent all their lives in a Welsh mining village came home one Sunday from chapel, where they had heard a powerful sermon on the faith that can move mountains. At the back of their cottage was an enormous slag heap, which completely blocked their view and was a constant irritation. One sister said to the other: "If faith can move mountains, surely if we pray hard enough we can get rid of this horrible slag heap." So they pulled down the blinds and prayed very hard that the offending blot on the landscape would disappear. When they pulled up the blinds again, the monstrosity was still there. "You see," said the older sister, "I knew all the time that it wouldn't move."

We need not feel superior and think that they should have known better, for on the face of it they were doing exactly what Jesus had commanded. Nor should we point out that obviously at least one of the sisters had no faith that their prayers would make the slightest difference to the slag heap. But neither Jesus nor his audience thought for a moment that this saying had anything to do with literally moving tons of earth and stone. Whatever else Jesus was, he was a realist. He did not talk about things that only happen in fairy tales as if they had anything to do with religion. But he was a master of picturesque illustration who told people to take the planks out of their own eyes before they started looking for specks in the eyes of their neighbors, who talked of those who were prepared to gulp down a camel but were so fastidious that they would choke over swallowing a gnat, who in speaking of God's care and concern for each of us said that our heavenly Father had actually counted the hairs on each of our heads.

By describing things that are impossible or incredible in this way Jesus arrested the attention of his Palestinian audience and made them think of the essential meaning behind his exaggeration and overstatement. So in this saying it would be quite clear to the listeners that Jesus was not really talking about mountains or, for that matter, about mustard seeds, which were proverbially the smallest of all seeds. He was talking about *faith* and impressing on the audience that even the tiniest particle of faith could achieve results that are comparable to shifting mountains. In Mark's Gospel (Mark 11:23) the same saying speaks of the power of faith as being great enough to enable a man to tell a mountain to throw itself into the sea, while in Luke 17:5–6 a similar saying uses the illustration of a man with the merest grain of faith being able to tell a mulberry tree to be uprooted and replant itself in the sea.

Moving mountains and planting trees on the bed of the ocean are things which are obviously absurd and impossible. But, says Jesus, men with faith can do things which look just as absurd and impossible. In the great eleventh chapter of the letter to the Hebrews we find a recital of what men of Israel were able to accomplish by their faith. But what is faith? Someone complained once that the word "faith" is a marvelous out for preachers. When there is something or other in Christian teaching which is difficult to understand—or perhaps when the parson does not understand it himself—he tends to say: "This is a matter of having faith," as if faith were a magic ingredient which we throw into a mixture of reason, experience, tradition, and Scripture in order to make sense out of life.

But this is not at all what the author of the letter to the Hebrews says about faith. He says faith means trusting in God despite all opposition and discouragement, venturing forward into the unknown future believing that God has a purpose for us and for the world, which in the long run he will accomplish despite all that the power of evil can do to thwart it. Or as Kierkegaard puts it: "Faith consists in a man's lying constantly out upon the deep and with 70,000 fathoms of water under him." Life is full of uncertainties, perils, and hazards, and in such a world the author of Hebrews says to us that the only certainty is Christ. Faith means believing that he was right, even if the devil and all his agents keep telling us that he was wrong. A German theologian has said this: "Faith is the assertion of a possibility against all probabilities. Such a faith has nothing else than Jesus Christ in the middle of a world which scoffs at all our hopes and fears." Like St. Paul we must be prepared to be "fools for Christ's sake" (I Cor. 4:10).

The author of Hebrews in his catalog in chapter 11 of Old Testament heroes who had the kind of faith that can move mountains, after mentioning great names like Abraham, Moses, and David, lists those nameless heroes who maintained their loyalty to God through hardship, persecution, and torture. He pictures them as taking part with us in the great race of life and together with us looking to Jesus, who himself has run the same race and reached the goal toward which we all strive, eternal life in the presence of God. But the story by no means ends with the Bible. Christian history highlights names like those of Francis of Assisi, William Booth, Wilberforce, Shaftesbury, Martin Luther King, Mother Teresa—social reformers, campaigners for racial equality, protectors of the underprivileged—who by their faith have moved mountains of hostility, indifference, antagonism, and hatred. It is surely an honor and a privilege to be enrolled in this great pageant of the church on earth and the church in heaven, even if the mountains we can remove are merely molehills.

# 4

## CHRISTIANS AND WAR

*All who take the sword die by the sword.*

Matthew 26:52

"THE CHURCH knows nothing of a sacredness of war. The Church which prays the 'Our Father' asks God only for peace." These words of Dietrich Bonhoeffer highlight the problem of the Christian attitude to war. Knowing that war is evil, many Christians have nevertheless felt in conscience bound to be prepared to kill others for the defense of the community of which they are members. Bonhoeffer himself felt it his Christian duty to take part in the conspiracy to kill Hitler, for which he paid with his own life.

The words of Jesus himself on the subject are ambiguous. Those quoted above were spoken in the Garden of Gethsemane just after his arrest. It seems to have been the practice for private citizens in the troubled state of Judea to carry swords for their own protection. On this occasion one of Jesus' disciples, whom the Fourth Gospel identifies as Peter, drew his sword and struck at the High Priest's servant, slashing off his ear. Jesus ordered him to put up his sword with the words "All who take the sword die by the sword." This is, however, not a command never to engage in fighting, but a statement of fact which had been proved true before Jesus' day and has been ever since.

What is undoubtedly the case is that Jesus and his followers in New Testament times were on the side of peace rather than war, but it is equally the case that they accepted soldiers, like slaves, as part of the normal structure of society, and regarded wars in the future as inevitable. But there is no clear guidance in the New Testament as to whether

Christians should or should not take part in war. Although there was some feeling in the early church that war was inconsistent with Christianity, there were many Christians in the Roman army, and since the days of St. Augustine the church at large has taken the view that Christians may fight provided the war is fought in a just cause. This policy is open to the major objection that in wartime both sides are generally convinced that they are fighting for the right and that God is on their side. The 1914–18 War was perhaps the classic example of this, and cynics have enjoyed the spectacle of Allied and German statesmen, encouraged by the chaplaincy services, exhorting the rival armies to lay down their lives for God—or *Gott,* as the case may be.

In the 1939–45 War the issues were undoubtedly clearer, and most Christians in the allied forces could take part with a clear conscience in a war against Hitler and his poisonous policies, which would have destroyed not only what Christianity stands for but what decent men of any religion—or none at all—have always stood for. Since then, however, the development of nuclear weapons, mass bombing, napalm, and other possibilities of genocide, prompts many thoughtful people who are not pacifists to ask whether the concept of a just war has not ceased to have any meaning, and whether taking part in mass destruction of life, which would be inevitable in any future war, has not now become impossible to reconcile with even the most elementary Christian convictions.

In an ideal world there would be no wars. Studdert Kennedy spoke for us all when he wrote:

> *Waste of Muscle, waste of Brain,*
> *Waste of Patience, waste of Pain,*
> *Waste of Manhood, waste of Health,*
> *Waste of Beauty, waste of Wealth,*
> *Waste of Blood and waste of Tears,*
> *Waste of Youth's most precious years,*
> *Waste of ways the Saints have trod,*
> *Waste of Glory, waste of God*–War!

However much those of us who have been in the service (as Studdert Kennedy himself was) would want to stress that war has other by-products such as comradeship, heroism, self-sacrifice, and compassion, no one can dispute the truth of his shattering indictment.

So the thoughtful Christian is faced with a real dilemma, which is evidenced by the fact that the same congregation may well have worshiping side by side convinced pacifists, who will under no circumstances take part in a war, and career soldiers in the Army. The pacifist will see it as his Christian duty to refuse military service—as Quakers have always done—and to engage in some kind of humanitarian work instead. The nonpacifist will think it his Christian duty to fight for the defense of his country against aggression, and to share with his fellow citizens the task of maintaining its freedom.

In the event of war, every Christian is faced in this, as in so many other complex problems, with a choice between two evils, to fight or to surrender—and each man must decide for himself which evil is the greater. Readiness to take part in a war means embarking on a course which in terms of modern warfare involves more horrible destruction than anything we have known; refusal to do so means contracting out of our obligations to the community, leaving our families to be fought for by others, and accepting the prospect of enemy invasion of our country with all its ghastly consequences.

All of us, pacifists and nonpacifists, will obviously be united in praying that a third world war will never come. But there is much that we can do in time of peace to discourage saber-rattling in our own circles, and to press for policies of reconciliation. The situation is not without hope, in that the two super-powers know full well that aggressive action on the part of either against the other would invite instant reprisal. It is in the interests of both to stop short of any action that would make another war inevitable, as in the case of Cuba, and to act as honest brokers in the quarrels among smaller nations, as in the Middle East. It is a fragile basis for world peace, but in the immediate future it is probably the most we can hope for.

When our Lord spoke of "wars and rumors of wars" as

being inevitable (Mark 13:7–8), he was speaking before nuclear weapons and genocide had become harsh realities. Now we know that mankind has the power to destroy itself but we also know that it need not do so. Christians can perhaps help most in the present situation by refusing to regard another major war as inevitable. Human sacrifice and slavery were once accepted as part of the pattern of life. Both are now unthinkable. Every day that passes without the outbreak of a third world war is a day gained toward the realization of Isaiah's vision that the time will come when "nation shall not lift up sword against nation, neither shall they learn war any more" (Isa. 2:4). Providence has been teaching us through the horrors of modern warfare that Isaiah's vision was no idle dream but sheer necessity for man's survival. It may be fulfilled sooner than we think.

# 5

## OUTCASTS

*I did not come to invite virtuous people,
but sinners.*

A FRIEND OF MINE told me that when he was a boy at
Eastbourne there used to be a regular parade along the
seafront on Sunday mornings after church. Everyone carried a
prayer book. This practice had two purposes. One was to
show that the owners of the prayer books had been to church;
the other was to show that they were the kind of people who
did not need to cook their own dinner.

The churchgoing middle class in late Victorian days,
and in the earlier years of this century, was in grave danger of
identifying piety with respectability. They regretted that so
many in the lower classes were addicted to wife-beating and
drunken brawls; however, if some of them belonged to the
humble poor who aped their betters and wanted "religion,"
they were encouraged to find it in the mission halls but not in
the churches. By the grace of God William Booth and his
Salvation Army lasses took Christ into the streets and into the
pubs, and reminded the churches that Jesus' prime concern
had been not with the respectable and godly but with the
outcasts and rejects of society.

The scene which Mark describes in his Gospel, and in
which this saying of Jesus is recorded, is reported also by
Matthew and Luke in almost identical words. It follows
Jesus' invitation to Levi, a tax collector, to become one of his
disciples, an invitation which the man promptly accepted.
He in return invited Jesus and some of his followers to join
him in his house for a meal with some of his former
colleagues. Nowadays it might be thought to be a mark of

16

prudence to be on good terms with the local inspector of taxes. In Jesus' day it was far different. *Publicani,* the "publicans" of the King James Version, were important contractors who controlled the taxation system in the Roman Empire, and farmed out the actual collection of taxes and customs dues to smaller fry, such as the Levi of this story. They had a bad reputation for extortion generally, and, in addition, in the eyes of orthodox Jews they were reprehensible because by the nature of their work they consorted with Gentiles. Hence they are bracketed in the Gospels with "sinners."

This social occasion which Jesus shared with such unsavory characters was reported to some of the legal experts or "scribes" who belonged to the party of the Pharisees—they would certainly not have been present themselves—and they took the disciples to task for their Master's outrageous action in mixing with riff-raff with whom no respectable person would associate—far less one who claimed to preach and teach in the name of God. Jesus' comment when he heard this was: "It is not the healthy that need a doctor, but the sick," adding the words of our saying: "I did not come to invite virtuous people, but sinners." Luke makes it plain in his version of the story that the invitation that Jesus refers to is a call to repentance (I have not come to invite virtuous people, but to call sinners *to repentance*—Luke 5:32).

Jesus' words are spoken with deep irony. The Pharisees regarded themselves as the "virtuous" people in society, and Jesus is not suggesting for a moment that they have no need of repentance. He is saying that his mission is primarily to those whose need of God is greatest, who are spurned by the respectable and made to feel that they are unwanted. They are the sick members of society, the down-and-outs and drop-outs of our day, the alcoholics and the perverts. Just as a doctor goes in among his sick patients to help and heal without fear of contagion, so Christ sees his work as the great healer of souls to lie with those who through their own folly or weakness are adrift from God. Far from avoiding them, he seeks them out.

So Jesus brings a city prostitute to her knees in penitence (Luke 7:36–50), and changes the life style of

Zacchaeus, the rich and crooked tax superintendent of Jericho (Luke 19:1–10). Yet his critics among the respectable people of his time denounce him for mixing with what they regard as the dregs of society, calling him "a glutton and a drinker, a friend of tax-gatherers and sinners" (Luke 7:34). But for Jesus these were still God's children, who could be transformed by friendship and sympathy into the kind of sons and daughters of God that they were meant to be.

Dean Inge once preached a sermon on the hardening of the spiritual arteries, which usually begins to affect us in middle age. We become set in our ways. We deplore changes in the church and in society in general. All of them seem to be for the worse. Particularly is this true of the changes that have taken place in the younger generation. They are scruffy in appearance, they lack respect for authority, they are undisciplined and ill-mannered. This is no doubt to a large extent true, and the mass media tend to encourage us to think that it is true of them all. Yet there has perhaps never been a time when so many young people have been so concerned in helping the underprivileged, the casualties of society, the social misfits. There is much less of the "holier-than-thou" attitude on the part of youngsters toward the "publicans and sinners" of our time, and much more readiness to stretch out a friendly hand.

Much of the credit for this must go to the sociologists and psychologists. They would not necessarily agree with the viewpoint of John Bradford in the sixteenth century, who, on seeing some criminals led to execution, exclaimed: "But for the grace of God, there goes John Bradford." They would express it in terms of genes, environment, conditioning, and so forth. But actions are more important than definitions; and the Jesus who condemned hypocrisy and Pharisaism in his time would surely commend these young people in our day who carry out his work. Is this not the sort of thing he meant in his picture of the Last Judgment (Matt. 25:31–46) when he said, Anything you did for one of my brothers here, however humble, you did for me?

# 6

## KEEPING THE SABBATH

*The Sabbath was made for the sake of man
and not man for the Sabbath.*

Mark 2:27

READERS OF J.M. BARRIE'S "The Little Minister" and similar
stories, or filmgoers who remember "Whisky Galore," will
know something of the rigid rules for observing the Sabbath
which prevailed in Presbyterian Scotland until well into this
century, and which to some extent obtain in the Highlands
and islands to this day. England endured the same restrictive
practices under the Puritans, and the Lord's Day Observance
Society reminds us from time to time of ancient by-laws
which are still on the statute book, banning normal weekday
activities on Sundays.

It is easy enough to dismiss all this as a hangover from
Judaism which has little if anything to do with Christianity.
The first Christians were of course Jews, who had been
brought up to regard the Sabbath as a day of total rest, on
which no work of any kind was permitted. When the church
moved out of Palestine into the Gentile world, and when
most Christians had no Jewish background, the Sabbath, our
Saturday, became an ordinary working day, and so for that
matter was our Sunday. The state arranged public holidays
with no reference to the seventh day of the week, or the first
day of the week, which had in Christian practice gradually
replaced the Sabbath as the Lord's Day, the day on which
Christ had risen. But Sunday was primarily a day for
celebration, when Christians met as and when they could for
fellowship and the "breaking of bread," the early name for

the Eucharist, in a spirit totally different from the somber atmosphere of the Jewish Sabbath.

Jesus himself had pointed the way in the incident which led up to our saying (Mark 2:23–28). As we are told, he was walking with his disciples through some cornfields on the Sabbath and, as they went, the disciples plucked and nibbled some ears of corn. This was permitted by the Law (Deut. 23:25), provided the corn was not cut with a sickle. The Pharisees, however, had included "reaping" as one of the thirty-nine activities forbidden on the Sabbath; and, choosing to regard the action of the disciples as "reaping," they challenged Jesus with condoning Sabbath-breaking. Jesus might have argued that this was the Pharisees' interpretation of the Law but not the Law itself. Instead, he quoted with approval an Old Testament incident from I Samuel 21:1–6, where King David technically broke the Law to satisfy the hunger of his followers. In Jesus' view, human need comes before slavish obedience to the letter of the Law. So, in this case, satisfying the hunger of his disciples was more important than strict observance of the Sabbath. "The Sabbath was made for the sake of man and not man for the Sabbath."

Most people nowadays would regard the second part of the saying as self-evident. Sabbatarianism, whether in Puritan or Victorian times, is rightly regarded not only as foreign to the spirit of Christ, but also as an encouragement to busybodies and killjoys, who deserve the condemnation which Jesus uttered against the Pharisees of his day. When Sabbath or Sunday or Lord's Day becomes a fetish, or a synonym for gloom, depression, and boredom, it serves neither the glory of God nor the enrichment of the human spirit. But that was not all that Jesus meant. Let us look at the first part of the saying, which is highly relevant for us in our time: "The Sabbath was made for the sake of man." Whether we call it Sabbath or Sunday, the "Sabbath-idea" insures that in every seven days there should be a day of rest, for relaxation, recreation, and renewal of mind and body.

It goes back to the fourth commandment (Exod. 20:8–11), which assumes a six-day workweek and justifies a seventh day for rest, on the grounds that the Lord created the world in six days (Gen. 2:2–3) and rested on the seventh, which he made a holy day. The thought of God working for six days and resting on the seventh was of course derived from the working conditions of the Jews at the time when the Old Testament was written. But even with a five-day workweek which most people now have, and even though we know that the universe took longer than six days to come into existence, the "Sabbath-idea" is more important than ever amid the pressures, tensions, noise, and monotony of life in a modern factory. In such conditions time off for rest and recreation becomes imperative if people are to remain people and not become as soulless as the machines they operate.

Jesus said: "The Sabbath was made for the sake of man"—and the institution of a Sunday rest has been the workers' greatest protection against unscrupulous employers. In the original fourth commandment in the Old Testament it is not only the head of the household and his family who are to benefit from the Sabbath rest, but the slaves and the beasts of burden. Naturally, in the complex conditions of modern society, the day of rest cannot be the same for everybody. Hospitals must function on Sundays, catering services must provide food, and even limited public transportation will cause many workers to have their "Sabbath-rest" on some other day of the week.

But the Bible would suggest one or two general principles. If we reject the interference of sabbatarians in our freedom to use Sunday for recreation and entertainment, we have also an obligation not to encroach on the freedom of others to spend Sunday as they wish, by involving them in Sunday work beyond what is absolutely necessary. For Christians there is an overriding duty to keep the Lord's Day in a special way by taking part in the public worship of God. In a sense every day is a Lord's Day, but Sunday is peculiarly a holy day, and the much maligned "Continental Sunday," which makes provision for religious services throughout the day—at least in cities—together with facilities for sports and recreation, has much to commend it.

# 7

## THE UNFORGIVABLE SIN

*I tell you this: no sin, no slander,*
*is beyond forgiveness for men;*
*but whoever slanders the Holy Spirit*
*can never be forgiven;*
*he is guilty of eternal sin.*

Mark 3:28–29

SOME MODERN PSYCHOLOGISTS tell us that there is no such thing as sin in the Christian sense. They admit that there is much antisocial behavior, but argue that it can be attributed to our environment, heredity, or even prenatal influences. The Bible, however, does not allow us to hide behind any smokescreen of this kind. It pins the responsibility for our failure to live as we know we ought to live, fairly and squarely on each of us. The Old Testament makes this shattering indictment of humankind: "The Lord saw that the wickedness of man was great in the earth, and that every imagination of the thoughts of his heart was only evil continually" (Gen. 6:5). The New Testament is no less trenchant. In St. Paul's words: "All alike have sinned, and are deprived of the divine splendour" (Rom. 3:23).

The most saintly characters have always felt their shortcomings most acutely. John Bunyan writes of his life before his conversion in these terms: "Sin and corruption would as naturally bubble out of my heart as water would bubble out of a fountain. I thought none but the devil himself could equal me for inward wickedness and pollution of mind." Psychologists would doubtless with some reason describe these words as the exaggeration of a neurotic, and most ordinary Christians would not speak or think of their past failures and inadequacies in this way. But without a sense that we have always been and still are sinners, the gospel message of God's forgiveness through Christ becomes meaningless. We are taught on every page of the New Testament that we must constantly be conscious of our faults and failings, but that if we are truly penitent God will restore the right relationship with himself, which we have broken by the wrongs we have done, and accept us once again as his children for Christ's sake.

The words of the first part of our saying are therefore in complete harmony with the general teaching of Christ and his disciples. "No sin, no slander, is beyond forgiveness for men." From the context it is clear that "slander" or, as the older translations put it, "blasphemy," refers not so much to maligning the character of another person, but to irreverence toward or defiance of God. Even this, says our Lord, is as forgivable as the normal sins we commit in the course of our lives. What comes as a shock, however, is the puzzling second half of the saying, that "whoever slanders [or blasphemes against] the Holy Spirit can never be forgiven; he is guilty of eternal sin." Jesus makes this doubly emphatic by introducing the saying with the words: "I tell you this" (or more familiarly, "Verily I say unto you"), which always indicate that what is to follow is of the greatest importance. Mark himself must have felt that Jesus' words needed some further explanation, for he adds a note in verse 30 to show that Jesus was referring to what had just taken place.

Jesus' healing ministry in Galilee, which included the sick in mind as well as the sick in body, had aroused widespread enthusiasm among the people. This was not shared, however, by the local Pharisees, who would appear to have regarded Jesus' actions as black magic, and to have reported them to the religious authorities in Jerusalem. A commission of legal experts, doctors of the law, or "scribes," was sent to investigate. They could not deny the reality of the cures, but what they could and did do was to attribute them not to the power of God working through Jesus, but to the power of the devil. They saw men healed of their various sicknesses, and men who were out of their minds restored to sanity, but instead of giving God the glory and acknowledging Jesus as his agent, they chose instead to accuse our Lord of being an agent of Satan (Mark 3:20–27).

This, then, is what rouses Jesus' indignation and provokes his vehement words. The scribes had been guilty of the one sin that is beyond forgiveness. They refused to admit that actions which were obviously good, and prompted by motives of mercy and compassion, were in fact good in themselves, because they disapproved of the person who was responsible for them. This, whether in the scribes of Jesus' day or in ourselves in our own day, indicates a state of moral blindness and perversity which in the long run could make us incapable of repentance and therefore put us beyond forgiveness. When we are prepared to call good evil we are on the way to damnation, which means ultimately separating ourselves from God.

Many good Christian people have suffered agony of mind because they feared they had committed the "unforgivable sin," thinking of such things as incest, betrayal of a friend, or mass murder by bombing. These are indeed grave offenses, but Jesus assures us that if there is sincere repentance, God forgives even these and similar crimes. The sin against the Holy Spirit, however, as the Bible makes plain, is not such an isolated transgression but rather a state of mind. And the frightening thing is that most of us are frequently guilty of individual judgments which are quite unfair to the people concerned.

We call good evil and sin against the Holy Spirit when we attribute unworthy motives to a politician promoting some worthy cause because we do not like his party, or to some social reformer trying to better race relations because we think "the blacks should be kept in 'their place,' " or to campaigners for improving the environment and securing a better deal for the underprivileged because we want a bigger slice of the national cake for ourselves. The lesson of Jesus' words is therefore that we must constantly keep a watch on ourselves, scrutinizing our judgments and analyzing our motives; otherwise our minds could become so distorted that we are no longer able to tell good from evil and become permanently the victims of our own fears and prejudices.

# 8

## THE CHRISTIAN BROTHERHOOD

*Whoever does the will of God*
*is my brother, my sister, my mother.*

*Mark 3:35*

IT IS IN KEEPING with the scanty references in the Gospels to
the "Hidden Years" in the life of Jesus that we know little
also of his family at Nazareth. The oldest Gospel, that of
Mark, begins with the account of Jesus leaving home at the
age of about thirty (Luke 3:23), and making contact with
John the Baptist's mission by the river Jordan. After his own
baptism at the hands of John, his public ministry began in
Galilee, and it is only then that we begin to get anything like
a full account of what Jesus did and said. But of his
upbringing, boyhood, and adolescent years we know next to
nothing, and can glean only such information as we have
where it is incidental to the main purpose of the Gospel
writers.

The saying we are considering here arises out of a visit
paid to Jesus by his family during his ministry in Galilee, but
Mark does not record it as a social call. It is rather part of the
picture, which Mark is building up, of the opposition which
Jesus' ministry aroused, ending in his total rejection by his
countrymen. Similarly, in the only other place in Mark's
Gospel where Jesus' family is mentioned (6:1–6), it is to
illustrate the hostility of his fellow-townsmen in Nazareth
toward the presumptuous behavior of someone who had been
the local carpenter and whose family still lived among them.
It was this that prompted Jesus' well-known saying that "A
prophet will always be held in honour except in his home
town, and among his kinsmen and family."

On the occasion of the visit of his mother and brothers, we are told that they had come down from Nazareth to the Lake of Gailee to find Jesus and take him home, since rumors had come to their ears not only of the crowds from all parts of the country that were flocking to hear him or to be cured by him, but also of the opinion of many that he had gone out of his mind. The brothers of Jesus may have shared this view (3:21). When they found him, he was sitting in a house surrounded by a crowd, and since, as Luke tells us (8:19), they could not get near him, they stayed outside and sent a message in to him that his mother and his brothers wished to see him. We are not told whether our Lord acceded to their request—presumably he did—nor are we told what passed between them. For Mark, the main point in the incident is that Jesus replied: " 'Who is my mother? Who are my brothers?' And looking round at those who were sitting in the circle about him he said, 'Here are my mother and my brothers. Whoever does the will of God is my brother, my sister, my mother.' "

Before looking at the significance of these words, let us consider a little further what Mark has to say about Jesus' family. We cannot tell whether he knew any more about them or not. In any case he would not feel that domestic details of this kind would be of great interest to his Gentile readers in Rome, thirty years or so after the Crucifixion. In our own case, almost two thousand years later, and with the modern interest in biography, we eagerly grasp at any crumbs of information which shed more light on the sketchy outline of the life of Jesus which the Gospels provide. Joseph of Nazareth is not mentioned as being one of the party on this visit, which has given rise to the common view that by this time he had died. When Jesus later went to his hometown and preached in the synagogue, he was as we have seen ill-received (6:1–6). There he is described as "the carpenter, the son of Mary," which does not necessarily confirm the fact that Joseph was dead, but may be an insulting reference. Mark may have known the tradition of the Virgin Birth of Jesus, although unlike Matthew (1–2) and Luke (1–2) he does not include it in his Gospel. The description of Jesus as "son of Mary" by his unfriendly fellow-townsmen may be an insinuation that his father was unknown.

The brothers of Jesus are named as James, Joses, Judas, and Simon. They seem to have been as unimpressed by Jesus as the natives of Nazareth generally, but James became a Christian after an appearance to him of the Risen Christ (I Cor. 15:7), and was to become head of the church in Jerusalem. Jesus' sisters are mentioned in Mark 6:3, but their names are not given, and were probably not known, or of interest, when Mark wrote his Gospel for Roman Christians a generation later. Much discussion has revolved around the question as to whether the brothers were children of Joseph of Nazareth by a former marriage, or cousins, or blood brothers of Jesus. Advocates of the perpetual virginity of Mary would support on doctrinal grounds either of the first two views, but the more natural interpretation of Mark's words would be that they were full brothers, and that Jesus was the eldest of the family.

Mark, however, concentrates our attention on what is for him, and for us, the more important saying of Jesus about his wider family. For Jesus, obedience to the will of God is fundamental. It is the test of Christian discipleship, and those who commit themselves to this way of life find themselves bound together in a new relationship to one another, which transcends the natural ties of any human family. When Jesus says in 3:33: "Who is my mother? Who are my brothers?" he is not making little of his family ties, although there must have been some tension between them and the one member of the household who had left home and embarked on the unsettled life of a preacher and healer up and down the country. A Christian family based on love and loyalty to one another can be an exclusive and even selfish group within the community. Jesus points to this danger, and calls on us to recognize our more important membership in the wider fellowship of all the servants of God and brothers of Christ throughout the world, who seek to do God's will.

# 9

## PARABLES

*To you the secret of the kingdom of God*
*has been given; but to those who are outside*
*everything comes by way of parables, so that*
*(as Scripture says) they may look and look, but see nothing;*
*they may hear and hear, but understand nothing;*
*otherwise they might turn to God and be forgiven.*
Mark 4:11–12

IF WE THINK of such well-known parables as those of the Prodigal Son or the Good Samaritan, it seems pretty obvious that their purpose is to get across the particular point Jesus wished to make, by telling a simple story to illustrate it. In the case of the Prodigal Son (Luke 15:11–32), it is to show the attitude of God toward the wayward son who comes to his senses and returns home in deep shame and apprehension, only to be welcomed by his father with open arms. It is clearly telling us of God's forgiveness for the repentant sinner. Similarly in the story of the Good Samaritan (Luke 10:25–37), Jesus is replying to the question: Who is my neighbor? by telling a simple tale which shows that our neighbor is anyone who needs our help. Instead of delivering a sermon on caring for our fellow men, Jesus chooses to make the lesson sink home by couching it in the form of a memorable illustration.

It comes therefore as a shock to seem to be told, in the words of our saying, that Jesus' purpose in using parables was to confuse and mystify people. This is so contrary to the impression we get from Jesus' teaching as a whole that we feel that something must be wrong somewhere. The setting of these words in Mark 4:11–12 is a typical scene by the Lake of Galilee where, as we are told, Jesus had to protect himself from being crushed by the crowds who had flocked from all parts of the country to be cured of their various ailments. In true Oriental fashion they clamored around him, anxious to be touched by him, or even by touching him to get a share of his healing power. Teaching in these circumstances was impossible, so he adopted the expedient of getting into a boat and using it as a kind of floating pulpit. From this vantage point he was able to address the crowd, and, as we are further told, "he taught them many things by parables." Not only is it unlikely that Jesus recited a string of parables as we have them in this fourth chapter of Mark's Gospel, but also as we can see from verse 10 he is at one point addressing a select group, while at the end of the day (v. 35) he is still in the boat. Mark is therefore giving us a selection of parables, which in all probability were spoken at different times and in different situations.

Jesus was not the inventor of the parable, although he was the supreme master of this form of teaching. Parables are found in the Old Testament, and they were commonly used by the Jewish rabbis in Jesus' day. If we want a simple definition of a parable, we probably shall not do better than take the one we perhaps first heard in Sunday School: "an earthly story with a heavenly meaning." This does not by any means cover all the types of parable, whether in the Old Testament or in the Gospels, but it is good enough as far as it goes. It suggests that a parable is more than an anecdote. It is meant to make people think. But whatever else they were intended to do, parables were never, in Jesus' mind or in the mind of any other teacher in his day or in Old Testament times, intended to be misunderstood as Mark 4:12 seems to suggest.

It may help us to understand the strange saying in Mark 4:12 if we look at the well-known parable of the Sower which precedes it (4:3–9). The details are familiar. Jesus may have been looking over the heads of the crowd at a farmer sowing seed. Much of it was wasted either through falling on the hard tracks which divide one plot from another, or through landing on the shallow soil that covered so much of the rocky plateau and producing corn that withered quickly in the hot sun, or through the young crop being choked by briers which had not been uprooted the previous year. Despite all this some of the seed fell into good soil, and when this happened the yield far outweighed the losses and wasted effort. The normal yield in Palestine was seven times the seed sown, and a good crop might be tenfold. But Jesus startles his hearers by saying that where the seed falls on the right kind of soil the yield is thirty-, sixty-, or even a hundredfold.

It would be clear to the listeners on reflection that Jesus was not talking about farming, but about his own message that the rule of God on earth had now begun. Despite opposition and much discouragement, he was calling on his hearers to have faith that from small beginnings God could bring a bumper harvest. Those who responded to God's call through Jesus to turn their backs on the past and embrace the new life were worth more than all the obdurate and indifferent who brushed it aside. So in verses 11–12 Jesus addresses the inner circle of those who had responded to the call—the Twelve and other committed followers. They had come to understand at least something of the message of God's love and forgiveness, and had seen the need to proclaim this in season and out of season, despite disappointments and apparent failure. They had grasped "the secret of the kingdom of God" and were ready to receive further instruction in discipleship.

For the rest, "those who are outside," the message must be presented in parables, in simple terms which they can understand, in the hope that they, too, in time might come to accept God's challenge. But let his followers not be discouraged. Rather let them face reality. The prophets had encountered the same problem, and Jesus refers particularly to the words of Isaiah (6:9–10—"as Scripture says"), who had had the experience of preaching to people who simply did not want to know. They were spiritually deaf and blind and, moreover, dull-witted. If this were not so they would respond to God's word and receive his forgiveness (v. 12). So, far from trying to befog his hearers, as at first sight this saying would seem to suggest, Jesus is putting his finger on a problem that still faces the church today.

# 10

## TO HIM THAT HATH SHALL BE GIVEN

*For the man who has will be given more,*
*and the man who has not*
*will forfeit even what he has.*

Mark 4:25

WHEN A MAN who is already well-off receives a large legacy, or wins a substantial sum of money in a football pool, one or other of his less well-off friends is almost bound to quote these words or something like them. There is usually a note of resentment, envy, or cynicism in the speaker's voice, as if to say that there is no justice in the world, and implying that this state of affairs must have divine approval since "it's in the Bible." It hardly needs to be said that because something is in the Bible, and more particularly if it happens to be said by Jesus, this does not mean that our Lord is in favor of it. He may well be condemning it. Many of his sayings are words of disapproval or criticism, as often telling us of things to be avoided as of things that we ought to do.

Jesus was more concerned with the use of wealth than with the possession of wealth, so that on the face of it he would not necessarily disapprove of a well-to-do person acquiring more money provided he came by it honestly. The current scandal of the land and property speculator, making a fortune by dubious, if legal, means, is a twentieth-century problem which will sooner or later be dealt with by amending laws. It was not a problem in the time of Jesus. But the gap between rich and poor was relatively speaking as great in Oriental society in those days as in the oil-producing Arab countries now. It may well be that the words of our saying were already proverbial in the time of Christ, coined by some cynic like Ecclesiastes who surveyed the contemporary scene with a shrewd and realistic eye. He perhaps thought of the moneylender amassing a fortune with little risk or effort, and the poor peasant dogged by bad harvests sinking into ever deeper poverty, but still having to pay the usurer his last penny. If this is so, the saying probably sprang originally from observation of one of the perennial and unpleasant facts of life.

But did Jesus use this proverb with any reference to money at all? It appears in chapter four of Mark's Gospel, which is a collection of parables all referring to the preaching of the gospel and our response to it. It would be unlikely that this saying would be about something quite different. The same words occur in Matthew 25:29 in the parable of the Talents, and in Luke 19:26 in the parable of the Pounds. In both cases the theme is about making money, but as in all parables, there is a deeper meaning. Most of us recognize that the Talents, or, as in the New English Bible, the "bags of gold," which the man in the story entrusts to his servants, stand for the gifts with which God endows each of us in varying quantities, and that what Jesus is saying is that what matters is not the gifts we possess but the use we make of them. We also recognize that the man who "buried his talent in a napkin" is the man who made nothing of his gift, who did not make use of the capabilities and skills which he had been given. So, in the story, his talent, or bag of gold, was taken from him and given to the servant who had made the best use of the money that had been entrusted to him. It is at this point that the words of our saying occur: "The man who has will always be given more . . . and the man who has not will forfeit even what he has."

The same saying appears at the same point in Luke's parable of the Pounds, and with the same meaning. It would seem most likely, therefore, that this is the context in which it originally appeared. Mark has found it in isolation in some collection of Jesus' sayings and included it in the fourth chapter of his Gospel, together with other parables. But whether it comes from the parable of the Talents or not, it has obviously nothing to do with the popular interpretation of it. Jesus is speaking of spiritual matters, not material things. We do not need our Lord to tell us that wealth begets wealth, by compound interest or shrewd investment. We can see this for ourselves.

What we do need to be told is that we grow in understanding of our faith and of God's promises only if we make the most of the insights we have received. It is in this sense that "the man who has will be given more." If by the grace of God we have been brought up in a Christian family and nurtured in the church, we have been given a priceless treasure and a foundation on which to build our lives. But we have to "grow in grace and in the knowledge of our Lord and Saviour Jesus Christ" (II Pet. 3:18). We have to deepen our knowledge of God, and enrich our spiritual life, by using the means of grace that God provides—sacramental worship, the preaching of the Word, private prayer, and Bible study. Most of us lead busy lives in an often puzzling and bewildering world. We need the inward strength that comes from a closer walk with God, and Jesus has pointed the way.

But there is another terrifying side to the picture: " . . . the man who has not will forfeit even what he has." Our knowledge of God will become a dead thing if through apathy or indifference we cease to listen to what he is saying to us. Our conscience becomes blunted, our vision of God is dimmed, our sympathies atrophy, our love grows cold. This is not something that God inflicts upon us. We inflict it on ourselves. Jesus offers us a choice—the way of life or the way of death. It is not a choice that we have to make once and for all. It is a choice we have to make every day of our lives as we respond, or fail to respond, to the challenge of the gospel.

# 11

## THE HEALING POWER OF CHRIST

*My daughter, your faith has cured you. Go
in peace, free for ever from this trouble. . . .
The child is not dead, she is asleep.*

Mark 5:34, 39

THESE TWO SAYINGS occur in the section of Mark's Gospel which the New English Bible calls "Miracles of Christ." The first one refers to the cure of an anonymous woman in a crowd surrounding Jesus during his Galilean ministry. She had suffered from hemorrhages (or as the King James Version puts it, "an issue of blood") for twelve years, and was instantaneously cured by touching Jesus' clothes without his knowledge (Mark 5:25–34). The second saying refers to the restoration to life of the young daughter of Jairus, the president of one of the local synagogues, which took place immediately afterward (Mark 5:21–24, 35–43). They both raise a variety of questions in our minds.

First of all, let us look at the two incidents in the total setting of Jesus' ministry. All the Gospels testify to the fact that Jesus was not merely a teacher and preacher but also a healer. A number of his cures are described at some length, such as the two referred to above, but there are far more references to large numbers of unspecified healing acts. This sentence from Matthew 9:35 is typical of many: "Jesus went round all the towns and villages teaching in their synagogues, announcing the good news of the Kingdom, and curing every kind of ailment and disease." This suggests that the cures that are described in detail are a selection of typical cases, which, however, represent a vast number of cures which are dealt with in these comprehensive statements. We

34

must conclude, therefore, that Jesus considered his healing ministry to be as important as his teaching ministry. It was certainly part of the claims made on behalf of Jesus by the apostles after Pentecost, that he had gone about "doing good and healing" and that he had wrought "miracles, portents and signs" (Acts 10:38; 2:22).

There was a time when the miracles of Jesus were regarded as conclusive proof that he was the Son of God. Then in the heyday of the scientific revolution of the last century, when the "laws of nature" were regarded as sacrosanct, it was held by many that miracles simply could not happen, because they violated the natural order. Today in some quarters the pendulum has swung to the other extreme. The healing miracles of Jesus, we are told, are reproduced daily in any city hospital, where bodily and mental ailments are cured by modern medical skills in ways unheard of before the twentieth century. This is simply not true.

No Christian would want to do anything but thank God for the advances in surgery and medicine, which alleviate suffering and make life more bearable for the diseased in body and sick in mind. All Christians would regard doctors, nurses, and those engaged in medical research as instruments of God's purpose in order that men and women—his children—should be freed from anything—beyond the natural onset of old age—which prevents them from enjoying the gift of life to the full and from contributing their quota to society. But this is not what the New Testament says about the healing power of Christ. The unanimous verdict is that, unlike modern medical practice, in the case of Christ's acts of healing there was no diagnosis, no prolonged treatment, and no period of convalescence. Cures were instantaneous—at a touch, with a word, or even at a distance.

Here we are in the presence of mystery—which simply means that we do not yet understand. As St. Paul says: "Now we see only puzzling reflections in a mirror" (I Cor. 13:12). But even now we have several pointers. One of them is our recent understanding of the importance of psychosomatic medicine—depending on the interaction of mind and body. We are just at the beginning of this. How can the mind influence the body and vice-versa? The Old Testament in its wisdom would say that both are part of the same thing. We are not merely souls hoping for salvation, but men and women looking for the fulfilment of our whole personalities, minds and bodies.

Another pointer is that scientists—like theologians—have become less dogmatic. They are much less prepared to claim that they know all the answers, and much more prepared to allow for the unexpected and unpredictable. Not so long ago space-travel, television, and nuclear fission would have been described as "miraculous." In this new recognition that we live in a far more mysterious universe than our grandfathers thought it was, we may perhaps be more ready to see the miracles of Jesus in a different light.

Jesus himself regarded his healing acts as evidence of the power of God at work in the world in a new way through himself. He offered himself to God as a channel through which that power could flow, and set no bounds to what it could accomplish. Thus, in the case of the woman with the hemorrhage, it was no magic associated with touching his robe that healed her, but, as Jesus says, it was her faith in him and in his power, which she believed came from God, that made her whole. Similarly, he says to the father of the little girl who had died: "Do not be afraid; only have faith" (v. 36). In this case it was the faith of the father in Jesus that set free the divine gift of new life. If Jesus had meant his words to be taken literally: "The child is not dead: she is asleep" and the child had been merely in a coma, no one would have troubled to remember the incident, far less to record it. Surely he meant that in the sight of God death is but a sleep and an awakening.

This is one of only three cases in the Gospels where we are told that our Lord brought the dead back to life. The others are the only son of the widow of Nain (Luke 11–16) and Jesus' friend Lazarus (John 11). All are cases of peculiar poignancy, which awakened the utmost compassion in Jesus' heart and induced him to exercise a power he rarely used.

# 12

## OUR TRUE SELVES

*What does a man gain by winning the whole world
at the cost of his true self?*

Mark 8:36

THESE WORDS from Mark's Gospel came immediately after
what might be called the turning point in Jesus' ministry,
and it is important to place them in this context. Jesus had
never in so many words claimed to be the long-awaited
Messiah, the object of the hopes and prayers of the Jews for
many centuries. Indeed, he discouraged the use of the title on
various occasions when it was accorded to him, since it was
obvious to him that the popular view of the Messiah in his
day was far different from his own. To most people then
Messiah meant a political and military figure who would
rescue the Jews from the grip of their Gentile oppressors and
lead them to victory, as Judas Maccabaeus had done two
centuries before.

From the time of his baptism in the river Jordan at
the hands of John the Baptist, it would seem that Jesus knew
that God had destined him to be the King-Messiah, but he
had become equally convinced that his Messiahship must be
peaceful and not warlike, and that his sovereignty must be
expressed in service. It has been said that the shadow of the
Cross already fell across the Jordan, but it had become clear to
Jesus during his Galilean ministry that the opposition he had
aroused on the part of the Jewish religious authorities could
only end in his death. It was against this background that
Jesus asked his disciples that most searching of all his
questions: "Who do you say that I am?" and got from Peter
the confirmation he had hoped for: "You are the Messiah."

Jesus had now to convince his disciples that victory and glory did indeed lie ahead for him, but that the prelude to it would be humiliation, suffering, and death. More than that, he went on to say that anyone who wished to become his follower must be prepared likewise to face death on a cross, the normal Roman method of execution. By the time Mark came to write his Gospel the first great persecution of Christians had taken place in Rome in A.D. 64. The mad emperor Nero made the Christians—including St. Peter and St. Paul—the scapegoats for a mysterious fire which had destroyed more than half the city, and which Nero himself was suspected of having started. Large numbers of Christians were martyred by crucifixion and many died other horrible deaths. The church in Rome was still shattered by this event when Mark recorded these words of Jesus in chapter eight, verses 34–38. They are a challenge to Christians to be ready to face death, if need be, as proof of their loyalty to Christ, to be willing to forfeit life on earth in the assurance of gaining eternal life in the presence of God. To seek to escape a martyr's death and hold on to physical life in this world by denying Christ, is to lose true life in the hereafter.

In the history of the church during many times of persecution, men and women have been faced with this choice over and over again, most recently and memorably in the prisons and concentration camps of Nazi Germany. The full story has yet to be told of the sufferings of Christians in Communist Russia who have died for their faith, and the pages of the history of the young churches overseas are studded with tales of heroic endurance of torture and death by Christians who have taken up their crosses and laid down their lives rather than deny their Lord, and who have gained the martyr's crown of glory. In the light of this endless tale of self-sacrifice for Christ and the gospel, is it not blasphemous to degrade the thought of carrying one's cross by equating it with an attack of toothache or a tiresome mother-in-law, as is so often done in light-hearted conversation?

But what meaning can these words of Jesus have for Christians who are not faced with this life-or-death situation? It has been clear to every martyr what Jesus meant when he said: "What does a man gain by winning the whole world at the cost of his true self?" or in the more familiar words of the King James Version: "What shall it profit a man, if he shall gain the whole world, and lose his own soul?" For them "the whole world" meant home and family, security and a peaceful life. All of this they were ready to sacrifice rather than be false to their commitment to Christ. It would have meant for them, as the author of Hebrews says, "crucifying the Son of God again—and making mock of his death" (Heb. 6:6).

The essence of martyrdom is self-sacrifice for Christ; and it would be effrontery to claim that any small sacrifices that most of us are called on to make, or are prepared to make, should be bracketed with the supreme offering of life itself. Yet in wartime countless thousands of men—and in the Second World War women too—have given their lives for their friends, for their homes and families, and for the community to which they belonged. Most of them would not have said that they were dying for Christ—not many people talk in these terms nowadays—but they turned their backs on all the glittering prizes that the world might have to offer, and chose instead the path of integrity and self-denial, which is the life which Christ commended.

And what of the unnumbered heroes and heroines of ordinary peacetime life, the mothers and fathers, sons and daughters, husbands and wives who spend themselves in the service of one another without thought of reward? Those, too, who devote themselves to good causes, to the relief of the needy, to the care of the aged and lonely, are in a real sense dying for Christ, taking up his cross daily and following him. Self-sacrifice, self-denial, and self-giving are the hallmarks of our true selves, the men and women that God means us to be. This is the abundant life to which Jesus calls us, compared with which worldly success, fame, and fortune are tawdry baubles, which end with our bodies in the grave. But a life lived in the spirit of Christ will never die. It has a quality that is eternal.

# 13

## TOLERANCE

*He who is not against us is on our side.*

Mark 9:40

BEFORE WE LOOK at what Jesus meant by these words we should notice that elsewhere in the Gospels he is reported as having said the exact opposite: "He who is not with me is against me" (Matt. 12:30; Luke 11:23). Surely both of these sayings cannot be attributed to the same teacher! But in fact they can, for both are true, and they illustrate the importance of never taking isolated sayings out of their context, but always interpreting them in their total setting. In the case of the saying quoted by Matthew and Luke, Jesus is being accused by the Pharisees of healing the sick by diabolical powers and not by the power of God. The meaning of Jesus' words in this case is that anyone who does not refute this charge and prefers to stay silent is as good as agreeing that the Pharisees are right. Jesus is asking his followers therefore to stand up and be counted.

The saying in Mark's Gospel on the other hand has quite a different setting and a different purpose. Jesus is on this occasion in a house in Capernaum, engaged in private conversation with the twelve disciples. John tells Jesus of an incident which presumably happened when the Twelve had been sent out on their mission of teaching and healing (Mark 6:7–13). They had come across a strange exorcist—not a Christian—making what John considered an improper use of the name of Jesus in driving out evil spirits. Exorcism was commonly practiced in Jewish and Gentile circles in the time of Jesus. Often it was little more than black magic, where the exorcist exploited the credulity of superstitious people by claiming to expel evil spirits by calling on such powerful names as Abraham, Isaac, and Jacob. Later even pagan exorcists used the name of Jesus in this way, and a magical papyrus has the formula: "I adjure thee by Jesus the God of the Hebrews." There is an illuminating example of the name of Jesus being used by Jewish exorcists in Acts 19:13–18.

On the occasion referred to by John, he and his fellow-disciples had tried to stop the exorcist who was using the name of Jesus—presumably having heard of our Lord's success in dealing with demon-possession—on the grounds that he was not a follower of Jesus: "He was not one of us," said John. We are told elsewhere in the Gospels (Luke 9:54) of another incident in which John was involved, and where he displayed the same kind of intolerance as here. A certain Samaritan village had refused hospitality to Jesus, and John and his brother James—whom Jesus had nicknamed Sons of Thunder—impetuously wanted to call down fire from heaven and destroy them, as Elijah was said to have done (II Kings 1:9–16). On that occasion Jesus had administered a sharp rebuke, and his reply here is similarly a condemnation of intolerance. Anyone who does Christ's work or acts in his name, says Jesus, is not to be discouraged, even though he is "not one of us" as John had objected. "For he who is not against us is on our side."

There is an interesting parallel between the sympathetic and friendly attitude of Jesus here to those who, as we might now say, do not toe the party line, and that of Moses at the time of the Exodus, as related in Numbers 11:4–30. To ease the burden of his responsibility for looking after the people on their journey to the promised land, Moses had been instructed to set apart seventy elders to assist him. Something like the pentecostal visitation of the Spirit came upon them at the time of their commissioning, and they became ecstatic like the apostles in Acts 2 or, in biblical language, they "prophesied." Two of the seventy were not present at the visitation of the Spirit of the Lord, but it was reported to Moses that they were nevertheless in an ecstatic condition in the camp and were "prophesying." Joshua, like John in the Gospel, wanted to put a stop to this irregular exercise of the Spirit, but Moses' reply showed the same tolerance as Jesus exhibited in our saying: "I wish," he said, "that all the Lord's people were prophets and that the Lord would confer his spirit on them all" (Num. 11:27–29).

The words of Jesus and Moses are timeless and we all stand accused. How ready we are to build fences instead of bridges, how quick to point out in connection with someone who is undoubtedly doing Christ's work and serving the community in his spirit: "But he is not one of us"—not a member of our denomination, worse still, not even a Christian. Exclusiveness and sectarianism have bedeviled the church throughout its history. We can so easily deceive ourselves that we are merely being loyal to our own branch of the church, maintaining hallowed faith and practice, taking a stand on matters of principle. So in their day Quakers have been cold shouldered by Anglicans, Plymouth Brethren by Methodists, Pentecostals by the church at large. Northern Ireland merely exhibits more irrational and cruel symptoms of centuries-old suspicion between Catholics and Protestants, fomented by historical and political accidents. Over the whole range of Christian witness throughout the world, the truth is that what we have in common is far greater than what divides us; and we are coming to see that this holds true also for Jews and Christians.

Jesus' words in our saying are all-embracing. Those who are not against us are on our side. He is not saying that one religion is as good as another, or that we should try to mix them all together and form a new one out of what they have in common. But he does ask us to be open-minded, to overcome our prejudices and to be ready to acknowledge the presence of the spirit of Christ in those whose beliefs we may feel to be unorthodox, or who may not call themselves Christians at all. In this sense we can honor and respect those who would label themselves humanists, Communists, or whatever, provided they are honestly seeking to promote the betterment of society, the relief of suffering, and a fairer deal for the underprivileged. What matters is not their labels, but their care and compassion.

# 14

## SELF-DISCIPLINE

*If your hand is your undoing, cut it off;*
*it is better for you to enter into life maimed*
*than to keep both hands*
*and go to hell and the unquenchable fire.*

Mark 9:43

THIS SAYING, followed by injunctions in the following verses to deal similarly with feet and eyes, looks like a macabre invitation to self-mutilation, calculated to appeal to fanatics and madmen. Notable instances of self-mutilation have occurred; the names of Origen and Van Gogh spring to mind. But even the devotees of literalism would hardly take these words as commands to be implicitly obeyed. We have already seen (ch. 3) that Jesus was a master of hyperbole, and that by overstatement and exaggeration he tried to startle his hearers and make them think. Another question raised by this saying is what Jesus meant by "life" in this context, to say nothing of the difficulty of the words about "hell and the unquenchable fire." Let us take these three points one by one.

First of all, Jesus is not talking about self-mutilation at all, but about the need for self-discipline. Our hand can be our undoing if it leads us to rifle a till or pick someone's pocket or forge a check. Obviously, however, the hand is merely the outward agent, prompted by a dishonest intention. It is this that must be checked. Similarly, our feet can be our undoing if they take us into places where we have no business to be. But again our feet merely do what we want them to do. Our eyes can enrich our lives if we use them to absorb the beauty of the world around us, and to savor the delights of good literature and great art. They can also be our undoing if we fix them covetously on other people's property, and allow envy to become our ruling passion—or if a lustful eye leads to illicit sex.

Jesus has been called both the Great Physician and the Great Surgeon. Here he is speaking as the Great Surgeon, calling on us to cut out any evil tendencies that threaten to ruin our lives. That means rigorous self-discipline and constant vigilance over our wayward thoughts. Self-discipline is not a fashionable idea in our day. The experts have been telling us clamorously for a long time that self-expression is by far more important, and society is now paying the price for listening to them, in terms of juvenile delinquency and distraught schoolteachers. We badly need a recovery of self-discipline among our teenagers too, but we cannot expect our pleas to fall on responsive ears unless we show clearly that we are serious about disciplining ourselves.

The down-to-earth writer in the book of Proverbs says: "Watch your step and save your life" (Prov. 16:17)— obviously good advice for mountaineers and less adventurous mortals alike. Benjamin Whichcote takes us a stage further when he says: "The greatest performance in the life of man is the government of his spirit." But B. F. Westcott brings us closer to what Jesus meant by "life" when he says: "The Christian is a competitor in a life-long struggle for an eternal prize." For when Jesus speaks of "entering into life" he means eternal life, life with God, beginning now, and fully realized hereafter. No sacrifice of our natural powers and freedom of action is too great, if it promotes a better relationship with God and avoids a guilty conscience. If we put ourselves under God's discipline we are no longer free to do as we like. We have to keep ourselves in check, restrain our impulses, exercise self-control. We may feel that in the process we are destroying part of ourselves, depriving ourselves of things that other less scrupulous people enjoy. But Jesus tells us that what seems to be a loss now is in fact a gain, for we have to think in terms not of this present life but of our life in eternity.

In these examples of the erring hand or foot or eye, Jesus is obviously not speaking of single or even occasional lapses. The gospel always leaves room for repentance and guarantees forgiveness. He is speaking of the corruption of mind and will into which we inevitably drift unless we take steps to check our besetting sins, whatever they may be. He tells us in forthright terms that our choice is between self-discipline, which fits us for eternal life, or going to "hell and the unquenchable fire." These are words that cannot be shrugged aside although they certainly do not imply the eternal torments of the damned, which figured prominently in Christian literature and art in past times, or in the "fire and brimstone" preaching of Victorian evangelists.

There are two Greek words which are usually translated as "hell" in English. In the Apostles' Creed, in the sentence "he descended into hell," the word is Hades, and means the state, condition, or place of the dead—quite different from the meaning of "hell" here. Here it is Gehenna, which literally means the Valley of Hinnom, just outside Jerusalem. In Old Testament times this had been the scene of the abhorrent practice of child-sacrifice under some of Israel's godless kings (II Chron. 28:3; 33:6). The Valley of Hinnom or Gehenna was thus regarded with loathing, and was used eventually as the dumping ground for the sewage and refuse of the city. It was, therefore, a place of crawling worms and maggots, and fires burned continually to destroy the garbage. So the name Gehenna came to be used as a symbol of punishment. Isaiah (66:24) had already spoken of the undying worm and the unquenchable fire as a metaphor for the destruction of rebels against God. It is in this sense and not in the sense of physical torment that Jesus uses these words in verses 43 and 48.

His meaning is therefore that we have a choice between self-discipline and self-destruction, but let us beware of thinking that we have taken the sting out of this saying by describing it in terms of metaphor and hyperbole. Jesus is in deadly earnest. He is talking of nothing less than the danger of being ultimately separated from God.

# 15

## MARRIAGE AND DIVORCE

*What God has joined together, man must not separate. . . .*
*Whoever divorces his wife and marries another*
*commits adultery against her:*
*so too if she divorces her husband*
*and marries another, she commits adultery.*

Mark 10:9, 11, 12

IT IS SAID that every third marriage in the U.S.A. ends in the divorce courts, and in Great Britain present trends seem to point in the same direction. Many would argue that this is a healthier situation than in the days when stricter divorce laws condemned couples to be legally bound to each other for years after the marriage had ceased to be anything more than a façade. On the other hand, even the most eager advocates of easier divorce cannot but view with misgiving the effect of broken homes on young children and adolescents, with their toll of insecurity and consequent juvenile delinquency. Of course, as everyone knows, a happy home and a respectable upbringing are no guarantee that a teenager will not go off the rails, get into bad company, and end up as a drug addict. Yet the evidence of the juvenile courts, social workers, and one's own experience seems to point to the fact that a broken home is more often than not at the root of the trouble when young people become drop-outs, or at best aimless drifters.

But if there are no children of the marriage and it has been entered upon purely as a legal contract, embarked on in a judge's chambers, it must be difficult for husband and wife not to feel that, provided the law of the land permits it, a divorce is a matter which concerns only the two people involved, and that if they find that for one reason or another they no longer wish to live together the best plan is to end the marriage and to try again with someone else. This was more or less the practice in Old Testament times except that according to Jewish law the dice were loaded against the wife, and while she could not divorce her husband her husband could divorce her on the flimsiest of pretexts, such as that her cooking was not to his liking or that some other woman he fancied had a prettier face.

Jesus would have none of this, and when he was asked if it was lawful for a man to divorce his wife—a trick question which was intended to involve him in the legal wrangles of his day—he at once lifted the whole concept of marriage out of the realm of lawyers' arguments and placed it firmly on the highest possible plane, as a contract undertaken by two people in the sight of God. He is saying that there are three parties to any real marriage, a man, a woman, and God. He goes back beyond Old Testament law to God's creation of men and women, and his purpose that in a new relationship with one another they should leave behind them the family circles in which they had been brought up, and become one, a physical and spiritual unity for the total enrichment of their lives.

This companionship which is part of the purpose of God for his children is obviously intended to be companionship for life. Divorce is thus out of the question. This is what is meant by the words of Jesus: "What God has joined together, man must not separate." He is not talking about whether the law has the power to terminate a marriage. He places the onus on the man who contracts the marriage. It is he who must not separate the partners in a God-given union. In Jewish law it was only the husband who could do this, but as the next words indicate, embracing the practice in the non-Jewish world, the wife who divorces her husband is equally guilty of sin in the sight of God. In the parallel passage in Matthew 19:8 there is the notorious proviso: "for any cause other than unchastity." Most scholars, however, regard this as a piece of Jewish legal casuistry out of keeping with the whole spirit of Jesus' teaching here, and not originating from Christ himself. It was probably inserted by some Jewish Christian who felt that Jesus' standard was too high.

Indeed it is for most people. Jesus is setting forth the ideal of Christian marriage, not drafting legislation for the world. We cannot expect those who do not acknowledge that marriage is a sacrament, or at least an institution ordained by God, contracted in his presence and blessed by the church, to treat it with the seriousness with which Christians must regard it. In an imperfect world the law of the land must make allowance for human weakness. But Christian men and women, as we know only too well, are also human and fallible. The church must therefore uphold the Christian ideal of marriage as a lifelong companionship, and condemn divorce as contrary to the will of God as revealed in Christ, but it must not be guilty of the same "hardness of heart" of which Jesus accused his countrymen. Its business in the case of a marriage which is heading for the rocks is reconciliation, not condemnation or repudiation. Christians must act in the name of the church to do what they can to hold a marriage together for the sake of the children of the marriage and of the couple themselves, by sympathy, advice, and understanding, remembering that the highest law of Christ is the law of compassion.

It would therefore be wrong for the church, or for individual Christians, to deny a couple whose marriage despite all efforts has irrevocably broken down, the prospect of happiness with another partner. Christ held up the ideal of companionship for life. It is no longer companionship if there is constant wrangling and bitterness for one reason or another. Things do not always turn out as we hope and plan, and if a marriage has reached the point of no return, common humanity, let alone Christian compassion, would leave the door open for a second chance—which is what the Bible tells us is God's way with his children.

# 16

## JESUS AND CHILDREN

*Whoever does not accept the kingdom of God*
*like a child will never enter it.*

Mark 10:15

THIS SAYING of Jesus occurs in one of the most beautiful scenes in the Gospels (Mark 10:13–16), made familiar by the words of the well-known children's hymn:

*When mothers of Salem their children brought to Jesus,*
*The stern disciples drove them back and bade them depart;*
*But Jesus saw them ere they fled, and sweetly smiled,*
*    and kindly said,*
*"Suffer little children to come unto Me."*

Probably it *was* mothers, but Mark does not say so. His account simply reads: "They brought children for him to touch." It could have been fathers, mothers, or older brothers and sisters, bringing the younger members of the family for a blessing from the famous Teacher and Healer. The disciples who "rebuked" them were not necessarily as stern and rude as the hymn suggests. They were probably merely trying to shield Jesus from a clamoring and importunate Oriental crowd and doing their best to give him some peace.

Jesus, however, was less concerned about not being disturbed than that the children should have his blessing. He was "indignant" with his disciples for trying to stop them from approaching him. "For the kingdom of God," he said, "belongs to such as these. I tell you, whoever does not accept the kingdom of God like a child will never enter it." Only Mark records that after he had said this, "he put his arms round them, laid his hands upon them, and blessed them." This moving conclusion, illuminating as it does our Lord's love of children, can hardly have come from anyone but an

49

eyewitness of the scene. We shall not be far from the truth if we think of this, like the reference to Jesus' indignation— also found only in this Gospel—as one of the many indications that Mark owed much to the reminiscences of St. Peter, with whom he was so closely associated in Rome, where he wrote this Gospel. Peter had been with Jesus and had seen, and remembered.

Although there is plenty of evidence in the Old Testament narratives of the affection of Jewish parents for their children, it is difficult to avoid the impression given by the book of Proverbs that corporal punishment played a major part in education. The author of the letter to the Hebrews quotes with approval words from Proverbs 3:12: "The Lord disciplines those whom he loves; he lays the rod on every son whom he acknowledges" (Heb. 12:5–6). Similar advice on bringing up children is given in Proverbs: "Rod and reprimand impart wisdom," "A good beating purges the mind," "Chastise your son while there is hope for him, but be careful not to flog him to death" (Prov. 29:15; 20:30; 19:18). This severe discipline of children appealed to our stern Victorian forefathers, who, attributing the contents of the book of Proverbs to Solomon, recited with relish—no doubt while administering the "rod"—

> Solomon said in accents mild,
> Spare the rod and spoil the child;
> Be he man or be she maid,
> Whip and wallop 'em, Solomon said.

Jesus' attitude to children was quite different. His affection, tenderness, and sympathy for them shine out from the pages of the Gospels. On one occasion when his disciples had been quarreling about which of them was the greatest, we are told that "he took a child, set him in front of them, and put his arm around him." The little child in its simplicity and humility was to be an object lesson to these grown men who ought to have known better, that true greatness consists not in trying to be important, but in service of those who are of *no* importance, as the world judges it (Mark 9:33–37).

In our present saying in Mark 10:15 it is not so much the simplicity or humility of little children that our Lord is commending, but their total dependence. This is the attitude that God wants in those who wish to enter his kingdom. But what do these rather puzzling words mean? Where or what is the kingdom of God? Is it something that we can enter now or something that lies in the future? Part of our difficulty is that we think of a kingdom as territory—the kingdom of Norway, the United Kingdom, and so on. But the word translated "kingdom" really means "sovereignty" or "kingly rule," so the kingdom of God means the sovereignty of God, and to enter the kingdom of God means to accept the sovereignty of God over our lives, and that is something we can begin to do here and now.

A small child is wholly dependent on his mother. When he takes his first toddling steps he knows that he will not fall and hurt himself since his mother is waiting to catch him. This, says Jesus, ought to be our relationship to God. We must cast aside our pride and our reliance on our own efforts, and accept God's help and guidance as a gift, recognizing that we are wholly dependent on him. It has nothing to do with a child's innocence. In any case, what child is innocent after it leaves its cradle? Jesus knew enough about children—and men and women—not to think of innocence as a possible qualification for a right relationship to God. It was after all sinners that Christ came to save. Rather he wants dependence, trust, and receptiveness, and tells us that if we approach God in such a spirit, we can experience that proper relationship here and now.

We must not be confused by terminology. The Gospels speak of "entering the kingdom." But sometimes, particularly in the Fourth Gospel, they speak of entering "Life" or "eternal life." Both expressions mean the same thing. Jesus said, "I have come that men may have life, and may have it in all its fulness" (John 10:10). He might equally well have said: I have come that men may enter the kingdom of God. But they must accept life—the kingdom, the new relationship with God—as a free gift of his grace, and trust him as completely as a little child trusts his parents.

# 17

## THE MONEY PROBLEM

*One thing you lack: go, sell everything you have,*
*and give to the poor, and you will have riches in heaven;*
*and come, follow me.*

*Mark 10:21*

ST. ANTHONY OF THEBES, brought up in a well-to-do Chrstian home, but orphaned at the age of eighteen, heard these words one day as part of the gospel reading in church. He took them as a direct command of the Lord to himself and forthwith abandoned his comfortable existence, gave all his possessions to the poor, and spent most of his life thereafter as a hermit in the Egyptian desert, attracting many others to follow his example. This was in the third century. About a thousand years later St. Francis of Assisi was equally moved by the same words and made them one of the rules of his order of preaching friars.

It has always been felt by some within the church that this is the proper life for all Christians and that if we take our faith seriously we ought to treat these words of Jesus as literally binding on all his followers. But is this what Jesus intended? Let us look at this saying in its Gospel context (Mark 10:17–27). Jesus in company with his disciples was on his way to Jerusalem, his last journey which was to end on a cross. He was accosted by a stranger, who is described by Matthew as a young man, and by Luke as a member of the ruling class. Running up to him the man knelt respectfully and, calling Jesus "good Master," asked the searching question, "What must I do to win eternal life?" Brushing aside the title of "good Master" as pointless flattery and with a sharp reminder that only God should be called good, Jesus went on to answer the man's question.

"You know the commandments," he said, implying that the way to life in the presence of God, which was what the man was concerned about, lay in keeping the Ten Commandments. Jesus proceeded to quote several of them, but as he later emphasized, they could be summed up in the two great commandments, to love God wholly and utterly and our fellow men as ourselves (Mark 12:28–31). The man's answer was that he had kept the commandments since he was a boy. Jesus fully approved of this and was instinctively attracted to him. But the man obviously felt that keeping the commandments had not brought him the peace of mind and the right relationship with God for which he was searching. His money had obviously come between him and God. As Mark tells us, when Jesus told him that there was one more thing he must do, sell everything he possessed and give it to the poor, and join the band of Jesus' disciples, "his face fell and he went away with a heavy heart; for he was a man of great wealth."

Jesus had put his finger on the man's problem and on his particular need—as it was later to be in the lives of St. Anthony and St. Francis. But it is not a summons to ordinary Christians today to embrace a life of "holy poverty." Few of us have great wealth. Many of us feel that our problem is rather to make ends meet. It would seem therefore that this saying of Jesus has little to teach us. But this is not so. The man in the story was not condemned by Jesus because he was wealthy. He was self-condemned because his wealth was his chief concern. On another occasion Jesus said: "You cannot serve God and Money" (Luke 16:13), and the New Testament writers frequently warn us to beware of avarice. "Do not live for money," says the author of Hebrews (13:5), and the first letter to Timothy tells us that "the love of money is the root of all evil things" (6:10).

In the sequel to the story we have been considering Jesus exclaims, "How hard it is for those who trust in riches to enter the kingdom of God!" and follows it up with the memorable saying that "it is easier for a camel to pass through the eye of a needle than for a rich man to enter the kingdom of God." Not surprisingly the disciples were astounded. Had not Abraham been a wealthy man, and the pious Job, they must have wondered. But Jesus' last word on the subject makes his meaning plain. Wealth makes it difficult for a man to be in the right relationship to God, but not impossible. The grace of God can move a man to use his wealth for the good of others. History is full of examples of rich men who have treated their money as a servant and not made it into a god. Hospitals, schools, churches, medical research, libraries, art galleries, and countless good causes testify everywhere to the generosity of those who have devoted their wealth to the glory of God.

But wealth is relative and we cannot escape our obligations by claiming—as most of us could—that by no stretch of the imagination could we be described as wealthy. Yet by the same token the citizens of the Western world are rich beyond the dreams of avarice in the eyes of the other two-thirds of mankind who live on the borderline of starvation. Press reports of spending-sprees on luxury goods, and the hectic pursuit of the pot of gold at the end of the rainbow via lotteries or premium bonds are equally repulsive to the Christian conscience. Stewardship of such money as we have is part of our Christian service, neither to hoard it nor to throw it away.

In the Welfare State much of our income goes through taxation to help the underprivileged, the old, and the sick. The tax system is a fair and reasonable way of fulfilling much of our Christian obligation to the community of which we are members. But we have also as members of the church an obligation to support its work as well, and to give generously as far as our means allow us to the variety of good causes outside the church which invite our help.

# 18

## CHURCH AND STATE

*Pay Caesar what is due to Caesar,*
*and pay God what is due to God.*                    *Mark 12:17*

THIS SAYING has been used to justify enforcing the law or breaking the law—as for example in the case of conscientious objectors in time of war. It was used by the German Confessional Church to support its resistance to Nazi policies, but equally by the pro-Hitler German Christians to endorse obedience to his anti-Jewish Aryan laws. It is therefore as open-ended as a Delphic oracle, which seemed to be counseling one thing but could equally well be understood as counseling something quite different. On the contrary, as we shall see, Jesus' meaning is perfectly clear. The incident where the saying occurs is recorded in Mark 12:13–17 in the precincts of the Temple at Jerusalem during Passion Week. Hostility toward Jesus on the part of the Jewish religious leaders was reaching its climax, and they only awaited a suitable opportunity to arrest him without provoking a riot among the people. Meantime they attempted to incriminate him by posing trick questions, in the hope that his answers would condemn him out of his own mouth.

On this occasion the *agents provocateurs* consist of a deputation of members of the Pharisaic party and the entourage of Herod Antipas, tetrarch of Galilee, who as we are told elsewhere (Luke 23:7) was in Jerusalem for the Passover. This unholy alliance prefaced their question with a flattering and completely insincere tribute to Jesus. The question itself was crafty and dangerous in the extreme. Judea was at that time under the direct control of the Roman emperor through his local representative, the procurator Pontius Pilate. As a symbol of their subjection and as a contribution toward the costs of government, a head-tax of one silver denarius, about twelve cents, was levied on the population. This tax, payable directly to imperial officials, was deeply resented by politically minded Jews as a reminder of their servitude to Rome, and by religiously minded Jews because the denarius bore the image and inscription of the emperor: "Tiberius Caesar son of the divine Augustus"—an affront to God and a violation of the second commandment.

The question, "Shall we pay taxes to the emperor or not?" was therefore loaded. If Jesus said No! he would have been arrested and charged with treason. If he said Yes! he would at once lose the sympathy of his supporters. He could not be the Messiah, whose first task, as the mass of the people saw it, was to break the yoke of the Roman oppressor. Either way the Jewish religious authorities would have achieved their end. It was a real dilemma for Jesus. He asked for a denarius to be brought to him. This would entail getting one from outside the Temple, since the idolatrous Roman coin was not permitted within the sacred courts. Jesus then asked: "Whose head is this, and whose inscription?" "Caesar's," they replied. Very well, said Jesus, "Pay Caesar what is due to Caesar, and pay God what is due to God."

This was not at all an evasive answer. It said several things: first, that Jesus was himself no revolutionary. He did not join in the battle cry of the Zealots, the extreme Jewish nationalists: "No tribute to the Romans." Second, it acknowledged Caesar's right to the tax. The coin was his. Let him have it! By using Roman coinage the Jews accepted Roman authority, and were therefore obliged to contribute toward the benefits of law and order which Roman rule conferred. But, third, far more important than what is owed to Caesar is what is owed to God—obedience, loyalty, service, the offering of our whole selves in thanksgiving for all that God has done for us. It is little wonder that Jesus' reply was received with astonishment. He had turned what was intended to be a political trap into a powerful assertion of the paramount authority of God.

We have often heard the cry: "Keep politics out of the pulpit," which usually means "Keep religion out of politics." Jesus will have none of this. The state has its place and function as our Lord recognized, and as later New Testament writers confirmed (Rom. 13:1–7; I Pet. 2:13ff.). The authorities are "God's agents," says St. Paul, and in his day the Roman empire guaranteed peace, justice, and protection for its citizens including Christians. Later, however, and still within New Testament times the situation changed, as we can see from the book of Revelation. Christians could no longer recognize the state as the agent of God. It was much more like the agent of the devil (Rev. 18:1–3). The state became a persecutor of the Christians, who could not pay Caesar what was due to Caesar, or comply with what the state demanded, because it conflicted with their prior duty to obey God.

This has throughout history since New Testament times been the problem of every Christian living under governments whose policies have been contrary to the will and purpose of God as revealed in Christ. The point has come for many Christians when they have been in conscience bound out of loyalty to their Christian beliefs to break the law. Yet here, as in so many other areas of conduct, there is no easy answer. Josef Hromadka, the Czech theologian, found himself able to cooperate with a Communist government, which was avowedly atheistic, because as a Christian he was sympathetic to much of its social policy. Other Czech Christians felt bound to oppose the government and ended in prison.

Many South African Christians have felt so strongly that the policy of apartheid is contrary to the will of God that they have defied the authorities and paid the penalty of loss of their freedom or banishment. Others, while deploring apartheid, have felt it their Christian duty to remain within the established order and try to change it by more gradual means. The Christian conscience varies in sensitivity from man to man and from woman to woman. We do not know how we would react to similar situations within our own society. All we can do is to hold fast to Jesus' word that our duty to God comes before our duty to the state and pray that if we are faced with such an agonizing choice we may be given the strength to act with courage and integrity.

# 19

## LIFE AFTER DEATH

*When they rise from the dead,*
*men and women do not marry:*
*they are like angels in heaven.*

JUST AS MEN—until recently—have always believed in some kind of God or gods, so also—until recently—men have always believed in some kind of life after death. As Martin Luther said: "Our Lord has written the promise of the resurrection not in books alone, but in every leaf in springtime." When death comes at the end of a long and useful life and an old person dies peacefully and contentedly, we can accept this as natural and fitting. But when children are snatched from life before it has properly begun for them, or when young men and women are robbed of their future in wartime by a chance bomb, or in peacetime by a gunman's bullet, or on the roads at any time, we feel this cannot possibly be the end of everything for them. So when a home is bereft of its breadwinner, or small children are left motherless, our questions are not answered by reminders that time is a great healer.

The ancient Egyptians sought to insure life after death for their kings and queens by mummifying their bodies and performing elaborate rituals in their pyramid-tombs for their journey to the other world. Partly because of this exaggerated cult of the dead among their powerful neighbors, the Hebrews in Old Testament times thought of life after death as a shadowy existence in the underworld, more or less like the Greek and Roman Hades. Gradually, however, toward New Testament times this was replaced by the idea of a resurrection. Unlike the Greek philosophers who taught that the body died but the soul was immortal, the Hebrews believed that body and soul were inseparable, therefore any life beyond death must be in terms of a bodily resurrection. This was the belief of most Jews in Jesus' day. Only the conservative Sadducees, who claimed that the idea of a bodily resurrection was a "modern" view and had not the authority of Moses behind it, refused to accept it. In controversy with the Pharisees, and in the case of Jesus' saying in Mark 12:25 in controversy with our Lord, who shared the Pharisees' belief in life after death, they sought to show that the whole idea of a resurrection was fantastic.

The setting of this saying of Jesus is recorded in Mark 12:18–27. He is accosted by some Sadducees who tell an unlikely story about seven brothers. According to the Law of Moses, if a man died leaving no children his brother must marry the widow. The first son of the marriage should bear the dead man's name and inherit his property (Deut. 25:5). In the fanciful problem posed by the Sadducees, the seven brothers died in turn, each having married the widow but leaving no children. At last the woman herself died. The question was: "At the resurrection when they come back to life, whose wife will she be, since all seven had married her?"

Jesus in his reply made two points, accusing his questioners of knowing neither the Scriptures nor the power of God. He meant that God can create new orders of life where the conditions are far different from those we know here. In the life beyond death, where death no longer exists, the physical side of marriage (as distinct from companionship), and consequently birth, finds no place. Like food and drink these belong to the earthly sphere. Life after death, says Jesus, is like that of the angels in heaven, a higher order of being where there is perfect communion with God. He then goes on to challenge the Sadducees' scepticism about a future life by reminding them that when God appeared to Moses at the Burning Bush (Exod. 3:1–6) he claimed to be the God of Abraham, Isaac, and Jacob. These early ancestors of Israel were by this time long since dead. Their bodies moldered in their tombs, but God was still their God. They were alive with him in his presence, for God is not the God of the dead but of the living.

Jesus shares the view of the Pharisees, as opposed to the Sadducees, that life after death is a reality, but he does not share the crude Pharisaic belief in some kind of physical resurrection of the body at the Last Judgment. He takes his stand rather with the Psalmists who were not satisfied that all that lay beyond death was a ghostly existence in the underworld (Sheol) beyond contact with God. On the contrary, the Psalmists expressed their conviction that a relationship with God begun here on earth could not be destroyed by the accident of death (Ps. 16:8–11; 49:15; 73:23–26). "Though heart and body fail, yet God is my possession for ever" (Ps. 73:26).

This is the basic conviction of the New Testament writers, illuminated and confirmed by their experience of the risen Christ in their own lives. They are not interested in *everlasting* life, in the sense of life that goes on and on after death and never ends. They are much more concerned with *eternal* life, life in relationship to God which has an eternal quality in it. For them death comes when we turn our backs on our past and enter a new life by committing ourselves to Christ. The death of our physical bodies is therefore incidental, and cannot affect our relationship to God. Thus St. Paul can write: "I am convinced that there is nothing in death . . . that can separate us from the love of God in Christ Jesus our Lord" (Rom. 8:38–39).

The New Testament gives us no encouragement therefore to speculate about the nature of the life beyond, except to encourage us to expect a deeper and more intense knowledge of God than we can get here and now. Since God is love, he holds our lives in his hand both in this world and in the world to come, where we shall be reunited with those whom we have loved and lost and who have passed on before us into the great fellowship of God's children in heaven. This is as much as we need to know. The rest we can leave to our heavenly Father.

# 20

## ANSWERED PRAYER

*Abba, Father, . . . all things are possible to thee:*
*take this cup away from me.*
*Yet not what I will, but what thou wilt.*

Mark 14:36

IN THE SERMON ON THE MOUNT Jesus says: "Ask, and you
will receive" (Matt. 7:7). This would seem to encourage us to
ask God for the things we want and to expect that our prayers
will always be granted. Our present saying in Mark 14:36
appears to contradict this, for Jesus himself asks God for
something which he does not get. The scene is the Garden of
Gethsemane to which Jesus has withdrawn with his disciples
after the Last Supper. It is the night before the Crucifixion,
and the words of Jesus at the Last Supper about his
impending betrayal by one of his own closest friends hang
heavily on all their minds. In the garden, in turmoil of spirit,
Jesus took three of his most intimate followers apart from the
rest, threw himself on the ground, and prayed aloud "that
this hour might pass him by." Addressing God by the
familiar Aramaic name for father, Abba, which any Jewish
boy would use in the family circle, he affirms his faith that
nothing is impossible for God to do, and then asks that this
bitter and grievous experience which faced him, this "cup" of
suffering and death, might not have to be endured.

But surely it is out of character, and foreign to the
whole spirit of his ministry, if Jesus is simply asking to be
spared physical suffering and death. The Agony in the
Garden was caused by more than apprehension of torture and
the horror of a cross. Many martyrs have gone to the stake,
confidently and calmly, their faith sustaining them. If this

61

was all that Jesus was concerned about, it could hardly bring about the "horror and dismay" Mark speaks of, or explain Jesus' own words, "my heart is ready to break with grief." His agony was assuredly much more the horror of complete innocence and perfect sinlessness being confronted by the awfulness of the human situation—the malevolence of the priesthood, the indifference of the masses, the disloyalty of his closest followers, the total ugliness of evil.

It is noteworthy that the author of the letter to the Hebrews fastens on Gethsemane, rather than on the Crucifixion, as the deepest point of Jesus' sense of rejection and dereliction. "In the days of his earthly life he offered up prayers and petitions, with loud cries and tears, to God who was able to deliver him" (Heb. 5:7). But then astonishingly the author of Hebrews goes on to say: "Because of his humble submission his prayer was heard." For surely the sequel in the Gospels is that his prayer was *not* heard. The "cup" of bitterness and suffering did not pass from him. He had to drink it to the dregs.

The explanation lies in the second half of Jesus' saying at this point. Having asked the Father to spare him this experience at which his whole being shuddered, he then went on: "Yet not what I will, but what thou wilt." If this was God's will for him he would accept it in humble obedience. His prayer was answered on the deepest level in that he was enabled to see what lay ahead as God's purpose for him. In William Temple's words: "God is perfect love and perfect wisdom. We do not pray in order to change his will, but to bring our wills into harmony with his." This was the supreme intention of Jesus' prayer and in this sense his prayer was answered. It was this self-commitment to God in perfect obedience that enabled Jesus to endure his Passion and to emerge victorious.

We cannot hope to understand the Passion and Death of Our Lord unless we see them in the light of Isaiah's words about the Servant of God, who through his suffering and death would save the world. Isaiah may have been thinking of the past history and future role of Israel after the Exile. His faith was that the People of God would yet be the means of bringing the nations to the knowledge and service of God, not by power and might but by their suffering on behalf of others. Yet we cannot read the moving fifty-third chapter of Isaiah without thinking that the prophet must have had some future individual in mind, who would embody the People of God in himself. However that may be, it is clear that from his Baptism onward Jesus saw himself as fulfilling Isaiah's prophecy. He was God's Messiah, God's anointed representative, who by his life of service, and acceptance of suffering and death for the sins of the world, would yet bring mankind to the knowledge of God, and would himself beyond his humiliating death be vindicated and victorious.

Jesus' prayer in Gethsemane sprang up from his dismay and horror at the magnitude of his task in bearing upon his own shoulders the redemption of the nations, and his acceptance of God's will in enduring the coming suffering and death was the crowning act of obedience. As the author of Hebrews says, Jesus learned that obedience to God involves suffering, even for God's Son, but because of his supreme act of self-sacrifice he was able to become the means of our eternal salvation (Heb. 5:8–9). Jesus was unique and his role in history is unique. But from his prayer in Gethsemane we ordinary mortals can learn how to frame our own prayers. The overriding petition, above all our private petitions, must be "Thy will be done," "Not what I will, but what thou wilt."

Whatever we ask God to do for us, or to give us, must always be qualified by the words "If it be thy will." When we do not get what we have asked for, it does not mean that God has not heard our prayer, but that his answer is No. It may be that we have asked for things that would not be good for us or that God has other plans for us in mind. Jean Nicolas Grou rightly said: "Speaking generally, it is true to say that the necessities and accidents of life form the main subject and the actuating motive of the prayers of the ordinary Christian." Then he added words which we may all take to heart: "One thing is certain: as long as you only pray to God for yourselves, your prayers will not be as perfect as he wishes them to be."

# 21

## SELF-RIGHTEOUSNESS

*Pass no judgement, and you will
not be judged.*

Luke 6:37

NO COMMUNITY can survive unless there is a code of law
which is generally accepted and observed by the vast majority
of its citizens. The more civilized a country becomes the
greater is the respect which is accorded to the law of the land
and those who administer it. Judges are highly paid so that
they may be beyond suspicion of accepting bribes, and
unbiased in their decisions. They are supported by an
elaborate legal system and an army of solicitors, barristers,
and court officials. All this is designed in order that
judgment should be passed on those who break the law and
offend against society. Yet that is apparently the very thing
that Jesus in this saying forbids us to do.

Tolstoi argued that Jesus was advocating the aboli-
tion of all courts of law, but few, if any, have agreed with
him. Indeed, if we look a little further on in this sixth chapter
of Luke's Gospel at verse 41, we find that the words of our
saying are followed by our Lord's memorable comment:
"Why do you look at the speck of sawdust in your brother's
eye, with never a thought for the great plank in your own?"
Clearly Jesus is not talking about judgment in courts of law
or about the public administration of justice, but about our
own personal relationships with one another. He is talking
about passing judgment on our "neighbor," our "brother."

But surely Jesus is not telling us that if our neighbor
beats his wife or batters his baby we should sit back and say
nothing about it to him or to anyone else. "Minding our own

business" is not a Christian virtue if it means ignoring evil things going on in our midst. If we discover that a house on our street is being used for drug parties or for distributing obscene publications, it is our Christian duty to report it to the police. St. Paul obviously did not think that he was misrepresenting Jesus' mind when he wrote to the church at Corinth: "Root out the evil-doer from your community" (I Cor. 5:13). This obviously involves passing judgment on him.

Jesus never pretended that the world we live in is all sweetness and light. On the contrary he saw his own ministry as a constant battle against evil—personified as Satan—and called on his disciples to take part with him in this ceaseless warfare. Inevitably this involves passing judgment on which causes, policies, attitudes, and people appear to be promoting reconciliation and good will among men, and which of these, on the other hand, promote dissension, hatred, cruelty, exploitation, and greed. There is no doubt about the side on which our Christian duty lies. In telling us to pass no judgment, therefore, Jesus is clearly not encouraging us to wash our hands of the world's problems. On the contrary we must take our stand on the side of right against wrong wherever and however we are called on to do so.

So let us look again at this saying of Jesus in Luke 6:37. In the same passage at verse 39 there is this curious saying: "Can one blind man be guide to another? Will they not both fall into the ditch?" It is not clear what is the connection between this saying and the one about passing judgment, until we look at the corresponding passage in Matthew 15:12–14. There it is made plain that the "blind guides" Jesus refers to are the Pharisees. It is therefore the attitude and outlook of the Pharisee that Jesus has in mind when he tells his disciples to pass no judgment, for the Pharisees were notorious for finding fault with those they considered to be less godly than themselves.

The supreme example of the Pharisaic mentality is to be found in Jesus' immortal parable of the Pharisee and the Tax-gatherer in Luke 18:9–14. As we are told: "It was aimed at those who were sure of their own goodness and looked down on everyone else." The story is that two men—a Pharisee and a tax-gatherer—went up to the Temple to pray. The prayer of the Pharisee was to this effect: "I thank thee, O God, that I am not like the rest of men, greedy, dishonest, adulterous; or, for that matter, like this tax-gatherer." He then went on to boast of his punctilious performance of his religious duties. The tax-gatherer on the other hand stood humbly in the background, beating his breast as a sign of his penitence, and saying: "O God, have mercy on me, sinner that I am." Jesus' conclusion was that it was the tax-gatherer and not the Pharisee who went home forgiven, with his heart right with God.

The sin of self-righteousness and censorious criticism of our neighbors is what Jesus means by "pass no judgement," and it is perhaps the sin to which Christians are most prone. There is a bit of the Pharisee in all of us. It is difficult not to pride ourselves on our regular church attendance, or our support for good causes, or our donations to charity, or our high moral standards, and by the same token not to cast a critical eye on those who do not measure up to our own superlative performance. In telling us to pass no judgment, Jesus is making a plea for sympathy and understanding rather than condemnation in the case of what we consider the shortcomings of others, who may be members of our own congregation, or who may not even call themselves Christians at all.

The Old Testament reminds us that "the Lord does not see as man sees; men judge by appearances but the Lord judges by the heart" (I Sam. 16:7). We cannot tell why other people behave as they do. We know little or nothing of their problems—the strains and tensions, the pull of environment and heredity, the financial worries, family anxieties, not least their state of health. Jesus urges us to look into our own hearts before we judge our neighbor, remembering that we all stand under the judgment of God. We cannot expect God to be merciful to us unless we are merciful in our judgment of others.

# 22

## GRATITUDE

*Her great love proves*
*that her many sins have been forgiven;*
*where little has been forgiven,*
*little love is shown.*

Luke 7:47

THIS SAYING comes from one of St. Luke's little masterpieces—not only in a literary sense but in its insight into the mind of Jesus and his love for the outcasts of society (Luke 7:36–50). It is a blend of incident and parable, beautifully told and deeply moving. It concerns a prostitute and a Pharisee, and it has often been popularly misunderstood in our permissive age as implying that casual sex was condoned by Jesus on the grounds that the woman had "loved much." In the words of the King James Version Jesus says: "I tell you, her sins, which are many, are forgiven, *for she loved much.*" The New English Bible translation of 7:47 given above makes it clear, however, that the "love" referred to has nothing to do with the woman's promiscuous behavior, which is on the contrary described as her "many sins." The "love" in question is grateful love, or thankfulness, or gratitude, to God for his goodness, as the Gospel passage plainly indicates.

The scene is a banquet in the house of Simon, a Pharisee, with Jesus as the guest of honor. If, as seems likely, this was held on a Sabbath after a synagogue service at which Jesus had preached, Simon had invited this traveling preacher, by whom he had been much impressed, and whom he regarded as possibly a prophet, to meet some of his friends. But there was in addition an uninvited guest who had also heard Jesus in the synagogue, and who had slipped unobtrusively into the gathering, a common enough practice for beggars or hungry folk who were content with the remnants of the feast. This, however, was not the purpose of the unnamed woman. Her concern was with Jesus. As the guests reclined at table, their unsandaled feet extended behind them, she knelt at Jesus' feet and, in an uncontrollable flood of tears, expressed her love and devotion and gratitude for his message, which had moved her beyond measure. She had brought a small flask of precious ointment, with which she anointed his feet after she had wiped her tears off them with her hair. In those days you would do this sort of thing to someone who had saved your life.

Simon was unmoved by this scene. His only thought was that if Jesus had been a real prophet he would have known what kind of woman she was and would have stopped her. Jesus, however, read his thoughts and told him a story. It was about two debtors and a moneylender. One of the debtors owed a large sum of money, the other a small sum. Neither of them could pay him anything so, uncharacteristically perhaps, the moneylender let them both off. Jesus then asked Simon: "Which of these two men will love the moneylender most?" Simon rightly replied, "Surely the man who was let off most."

Jesus' use of the word "love" is odd in this context. We should have expected something like: Which of the two men will be most grateful? And indeed linguistic experts tell us that there is no word in Hebrew, Aramaic, or Syriac for "thank" or "thankfulness." The word "love" is used instead. What Jesus meant therefore was: Which of the two men will feel the deepest thankfulness? This makes more sense both of the parable and of its application in the case of the woman, for it indicates that throughout this passage, and especially in the saying we are considering, it is not "love" that Jesus is speaking about but "gratitude."

He then goes on to contrast the behavior of his host the Pharisee with that of the uninvited guest. Simon had not even provided the normal courtesies accorded to a visitor: a basin of water to wash the dust off his feet, a kiss of welcome, a few drops of common oil to anoint his forehead as a mark of esteem. The woman, whom Simon regarded as beyond the pale, had bathed Jesus' feet with her tears and dried them with her hair; she had never stopped kissing his feet, and had anointed them with precious perfume.

Jesus in his sermon in the synagogue must have declared God's forgiveness of all penitent sinners. The woman had taken this to herself and had sought out Jesus, overwhelmed with thankfulness. Her deep gratitude as evidenced by her actions was proof that her sins had been forgiven. Simon, the virtuous Pharisee, knew less of God's forgiving love than the poor prostitute, who was now closer to God than this righteous ecclesiastic. Her thankfulness like that of the man in the parable who had been let off the larger debt was incomparably greater, because the burden of her "many sins" had been lifted from her shoulders. The Pharisee, who felt he had done little or nothing that needed God's forgiveness, had no such sense of gratitude. He may have kept all the commandments, but if he was thankful to God it may have been as in the case of the other Pharisee about whom Jesus told a story, thankfulness that he was not like the rest of men (Luke 18:11).

The climax of the incident described in Luke 7:36–50 is that Jesus gives the woman formal absolution, a confirmation that her past sins have indeed been blotted out. Despite the indignant muttering among the other guests as to this peasant-preacher's right to forgive sins, Jesus assures the woman in almost the same words as he used to the woman with the hemorrhage (Mark 5:34; Luke 8:48): "Your faith has saved you; go in peace." The whole passage sheds much light on our Lord himself—his readiness to take part in such social occasions, his quick sympathy with the sinner, and his willingness to forgive the sin. But it also shows us in a real-life situation the value he placed on true gratitude to God for his gift of new life, and, by contrast, his disapproval of rigidly moral behavior which leaves little room for the warmth of human feeling and compassion for the unfortunate.

# 23

## RENOUNCING THE WORLD

*Leave the dead to bury their dead;*
*you must go and announce the kingdom of God. . . .*
*No one who sets his hand to the plough*
*and then keeps looking back*
*is fit for the kingdom of God.*

*Luke 9:60, 62*

WE HAVE ALREADY SEEN (ch. 8) that Jesus points his
followers beyond the natural ties of love and affection that
bind a family together, to that wider fellowship of the church
in which we are all brothers and sisters of Christ. As we saw
then, our Lord did not make light of family relationships,
but sought to place them in a more far-reaching context.
Here on the other hand are two sayings of Jesus, both
concerned with our obligations to our families, which appear
at first sight to be extremely harsh and unsympathetic.

The theme is the same although two different men
are involved. Both are concerned with discipleship. Jesus
summons the first man to his service with the words: "Follow
me." The man asks leave to bury his father first but is
peremptorily told: "Leave the dead to bury their dead," and
is further told that he must go and announce the kingdom of
God. The second man seems to have been similarly told to
join the band of Jesus' followers, but asks permission to say
good-bye to his family first. This apparently harmless and
natural request is dismissed with words to the effect that
anyone setting out to plough a field and constantly looking
back, instead of looking forward and concentrating on his
job, is unfit to be Christ's follower.

The Jesus of the Gospels is neither unsympathetic to human feelings nor unreasonable in his demands. In the Old Testament there is a similar story where Elijah summons Elisha to become his disciple, and when Elisha asks for leave to return home to take farewell of his family first, the request is granted (I Kings 19:19–21). We must therefore look for special grounds for what seems to be a more callous attitude on the part of Jesus. And indeed if we see this incident in the context of Jesus' whole ministry and plan of campaign much becomes plain.

Jesus was approaching the close of his Galilean ministry. He was already bent on throwing out the challenge to the established authorities in Jerusalem which he knew was bound to end in his death. He had hoped that his message would gradually win men's hearts and minds, and make them ready to commit their lives to the service of God. This had not happened. Instead there had been apathy, misunderstanding, and opposition. He had therefore resolved to concentrate on a nucleus of chosen followers, men who would give up everything to become a spearhead of attack, a task force of evangelistic mission—preaching and healing—confronting people with God's demands and calling for decision. The time left to him to create this new Israel was all too short. Consequently nothing but absolute renunciation of all natural and material ties would qualify a man to belong to this chosen band, and in the following chapter of Luke's Gospel we are told how Jesus sent out seventy of his disciples in pairs to prepare the way for his own mission.

Jesus was therefore involved at this time in a process of sifting out a small group who would be totally and unconditionally committed to this missionary task, much in the manner—although the circumstances were different—that Gideon picked his fighting force of three hundred out of the thirty-two thousand who were loosely attached to him (Judg. 7:1–8). In the Middle Ages St. Francis of Assisi followed the example of Jesus in demanding total renunciation of secular attachments and ambitions from his Grey Friars as he sent them out to preach the gospel, and, like Jesus, Francis himself set the pattern for his disciples.

In the light of this let us look again at the words of Jesus in this passage in Luke 9:60–62. We do not know enough about the circumstances to say whether the first man's father was already dead, awaiting burial, or whether the man wanted to put off his assignment until his father had died. In either case Jesus' words about leaving the dead to bury their dead would mean that there were plenty of others who were spiritually dead, i.e., who had not been seized by the importance and urgency of Jesus' mission. To them could be left the normal arrangements for burial. The man in question was being summoned to a task which must be ranked second to none and which brooked no delay. Similarly, in his reply to the man who wanted to take farewell of his people at home, Jesus is simply forcefully asserting the primary duty of a committed disciple to put the service of God before any personal considerations and family loyalties.

But having recognized that this demand of Jesus for total renunciation of all earthly ties was designed to meet a particular situation—the creation of a tightly knit band of men who could be trusted to carry on the Lord's work after his death—have we merely succeeded in making a hard saying easy by limiting its challenge to the men of Christ's own time? This is far from true. From its earliest days the church has always recognized that the normal life of a Christian man or woman will involve family relationships, earning a living, providing for children, and taking part in the life of the wider community, with all the imperfections and compromises that that involves. There have always been some, however— in religious orders, in missionary enterprises, in nursing service, in social work—who have heeded the call for renunciation of normal attachments and who have kept before our eyes the ideal of total discipleship as an inspiration and a challenge. The church would be a pale shadow of its true self without them. But more than that, these words of Jesus would say to all of us that Christian discipleship involves self-discipline and self-denial and means constant examination of our motives. Christ's service is not something to be entered upon lightheartedly. We have to count the cost.

# 24

## THE PROBLEM OF PAIN

*The eighteen people who were killed*
*when the tower fell on them at Siloam—*
*do you imagine they were more guilty*
*than all the other people living in Jerusalem?*

*Luke 13:4*

IN THE LITANY we pray to be delivered from "sudden death" such as overtook the victims of the disaster Jesus refers to in this saying. The point of the petition in the Litany is presumably the fear of being caught unprepared without any time being allowed us to make our peace with God. In our own day people are less concerned about being overtaken by sudden death than about lingering perhaps for years with some painful illness. We often hear it said: "When it's my turn to go I hope it happens quickly."

It is, however, the wider aspect of suffering and death which our saying deals with. The problem is older than the book of Job, but it is in that book that the question is most fully handled in the Bible. Why do innocent people suffer? The orthodox answer in Old Testament times was that all suffering, including death, is the result of sin. Anyone whose life was cut short, or who was afflicted by some disease, must have done something to deserve it. When Ezekiel said: "The soul that sins shall die" (Ezek. 18:4), he was protesting against the practice of holding a tribe or a whole family responsible for the crime of one of its members. He was rightly insisting that only the individual concerned should be punished.

This had come to be misunderstood, however, and it was turned the other way around to imply that those who

73

suffered death or disaster must be guilty of some grievous sin. The author of the book of Job wrote his masterpiece in protest against this obviously unjust doctrine, by describing a man who was innocent of any crimes, but who suffered appallingly in mind and body, yet who insisted to the last that he was not guilty. Despite the book of Job, the view was still widely held in Jesus' day that suffering implied guilt, and that such divine retribution was visited on evildoers only.

The situation outlined at the beginning of chapter thirteen of Luke's Gospel (vv. 1–5) refers to two cases of sudden death. The first was a brutal massacre of some Galileans in the Temple at Jerusalem, while they were engaged in offering sacrifices. This took place on the orders of Pilate, the Roman governor, who must have suspected an insurrection, and was determined to nip it in the bud. The second was an accident which involved the deaths of eighteen people, presumably workmen engaged in repairs to the tower of Siloam, which collapsed on top of them. The implied question to Jesus was, What crime had these two groups of victims committed so that they suffered this tragic fate?

In both cases Jesus dismisses the suggestion that the men involved were more sinful than the others who escaped death. He refuses to accept the popular idea that disasters and calamities are God's punishment for sins committed by the victims. He assumes the fact that no man is completely guiltless. All men are sinful, and should take such tragedies as a warning. "Unless you repent, you will all of you come to the same end." This of course does not mean that all of us will be massacred, or crushed by falling masonry. Jesus means that life is a serious business, and we never know when we shall be called to face our Maker. It therefore behooves us to live in such a way that, when the time comes, we can be unafraid and unashamed. Since we are all sinners this means making our peace with God daily in confession and penitence and not leaving it for some deathbed repentance. We may not be given time.

But as well as being a word of warning, Jesus' saying is a word of liberation. For we still find people today, and indeed to some extent it is true of all of us, who tend to think of God as meting out punishments in terms of hardships and misfortunes. What have I done to deserve this? says a man who contracts polio or is stricken with blindness. It is true that some suffering is caused by our own sin—by abuse of drugs or alcohol, for example. It is also true that some suffering is caused by the sins of society as a whole—such as malnutrition or pollution, which can be traced to man's greed or irresponsibility. But there are natural disasters which cause havoc and loss of life—storms at sea, earthquakes, tornadoes, and the like—which cannot be laid at anyone's door. We call these "acts of God."

This is rather for lack of a better explanation; and if we take Jesus' words seriously, the suffering and deaths that are the result of these "acts of God" have nothing to do with the innocence or guilt of the people involved. Jesus does not embark on any attempt to give an answer in terms of philosophy to the problem of pain any more than he gives us any philosophical arguments for the existence of God. We have to recognize that there are some questions that are ultimately unanswerable because of the limitations of the human mind. Why some should be afflicted with incurable diseases and others not, why some should go through life trouble-free and die at a ripe old age peacefully in their beds, while others are untimely snatched from life both in peace and war, to such problems we may one day know the answer, but certainly not in this world. In George Tyrrell's wise words: "There is ever a Beyond of mystery; for the more we know, the more we wonder."

Jesus, however, does assure us that in the matter of individual disasters and sudden death, the question of individual sin or guilt does not arise, and in the case of suffering he has left us an example of how to bear it. Suffering patiently borne as we well know can be an inspiration to a family or indeed to a whole community. "Christ has given us an example," said Cardinal Newman, "that we may follow in his steps. He went through far more, infinitely more, than we can be called to suffer. Our brethren have gone through much more; and they seem to encourage us by their success, and to sympathize in our essay. Now it is our turn."

# 25

## REPENTANCE

*There will be greater joy in heaven
over one sinner who repents
than over ninety-nine righteous people
who do not need to repent.*

THE FIFTEENTH CHAPTER of St. Luke's Gospel contains three stories that Jesus told to illustrate the forgiving love of God. They concern a Lost Sheep, a Lost Coin, and a Lost Son (better known as the Prodigal Son). The saying in verse 7 quoted here comes from the story of the Lost Sheep. Jesus had been adversely criticized once again by some local pillars of respectability for mixing with unsavory characters. He tells them a homely tale of a shepherd who finds that one of his hundred sheep is missing. He leaves the other ninety-nine in the safety of the fold and goes off to search for the stray, not resting until he finds it. His delight is unbounded when at last the wanderer is located. Hoisting it on to his shoulders he returns home, and summons his friends and neighbors to rejoice with him that he has found his lost sheep. The climax of the parable is the saying we are now concerned with. Jesus makes it plain that the lost sheep in his story is like one of the outcasts of society, whose presence among them the respectable people so much resent, but goes on to say that the recovery of one of them brings more joy to the heart of God than ninety-nine faithful folk who have never strayed from the path of virtue.

What is puzzling about Jesus' actual words on this occasion is that he speaks of the sinner who repents and the

76

righteous who do not need to repent, using the same word for repentance in both cases. But surely the whole teaching of the Bible underlines the fact that we are all sinners and all need to repent! Every Sunday at the Eucharist we are invited to repent and confess our sins, and are assured that if we have "hearty repentance and true faith" and turn to God, he will pardon and deliver us from all our sins. It is thus assumed in the Prayer Book that all of us in fact need to repent, yet Jesus seems to be saying that it is only one in a hundred who needs to do so.

St. Mark tells us that the burden of Jesus' message during his Galilean ministry was "repent and believe" (Mark 1:15). By "repent" he obviously meant something more than regret for past peccadilloes. He meant that men should turn their backs upon their past—their sinful, selfish, aimless past, with its record of failure, frustration, and folly—and turn their faces toward God in faith and commitment. It means a reorientation of the whole personality, becoming God-centered instead of self-centered, becoming "converted"—which for most people is not sudden, but is rather a lifelong process. It is something we do not do for ourselves but God does for us, and much of it happens unconsciously as we avail ourselves of the means of grace provided for us in the worship of the church—in prayer and sacrament, in the preaching and hearing of God's word in Holy Scripture.

Clearly, then, this major and decisive act of committing our lives to God involves a greater degree of repentance than the repentance we feel every time we say the Lord's Prayer and ask for forgiveness, or when we join in the general confession. When Jesus speaks of the ninety-nine righteous people who do not need to repent he is therefore speaking relatively and not absolutely. He would not tell us to pray for God's forgiveness in the Lord's Prayer if we had nothing to repent of. We know ourselves only too well not to be conscious of our daily failure to live as we ought to live, and of how much we need the help of the God to whom all hearts are open, and from whom no screts are hid, to cleanse the thoughts of our hearts.

Isaiah promised in the name of God: "Though your sins are scarlet, they may become white as snow" (1:18); and William Temple said, rather sadly perhaps, "My sins are not scarlet, they are grey—all grey." In the eyes of the Pharisees to whom Jesus told the story of the Lost Sheep it was the "scarlet" sins of the bad characters who had flocked to listen to Jesus which disturbed them—moral laxity, dishonesty, and the like. Their own sins—self-righteousness, censoriousness, intolerance (the "grey" sins)—did not count. In their view they belonged to the ninety-nine righteous people who, as Jesus implies, do not think they need to repent.

There is a story told of a mission service in a city church at which the visiting preacher had spoken admirably and truly—but without passion—of God's care and concern for all his creatures. A woman who had drifted in from the street, obviously in turmoil of spirit and impatient at what she felt was a discourse that skimmed the surface of her problem, leaned over the gallery and called out: "Mister, your rope's not long enough to save folks like me." Her need was to be told of a God who goes out to find the single lost sheep who has strayed from the fold, not just a benevolent Creator who is well disposed to us all. So the picture of the Good Shepherd with the sheep on his shoulders or the lamb in his arms has always been a powerful and moving symbol of the love of God which seeks out the sinner and welcomes him back to the family circle.

Jesus came to save sinners whose sins are scarlet and whose encounter with him turns despair into hope and opens the way to a new life. Those of us whose sins are "grey, all grey," have the same need for repentance and forgiveness, and for cleansing from the dust of the way—the daily failures, the harsh judgments, the selfish impulses. As P. T. Forsyth wisely said: "It is not the sins that damn but the sin into which sins settle down."

# 26

## SINGLE-MINDEDNESS

*The worldly are more astute than the other-worldly
in dealing with their own kind.*

*Luke 16:8*

TAKEN OUT OF THEIR CONTEXT these words of Jesus tell us
nothing that we do not already know. Astuteness and
financial expertise have never been reckoned to be attributes
of pastors, for example, who are expected to be concerned
about "higher things." In church affairs "the other-worldly,"
whether in holy orders or not, are respected for their piety, or
learning, or pastoral concern, or kindliness, but the raising of
funds, maintenance of fabric, insurance of property, and such
like are generally felt to be better left in the hands of
competent businessmen among the laity who put their
talents at the disposal of the church, and render invaluable
service by their knowledge of the world and its ways and their
practical approach to matters involving money.

But seen in their context Jesus' words present us with
a problem, because he seems to be commending plain
dishonesty or at best a dubious financial "fiddle." The saying
quoted above comes from the sixteenth chapter of St. Luke's
Gospel and forms the conclusion of a parable whose chief
character is variously described as "The Unjust Steward,"
"The Dishonest Steward," or "The Clever Rascal" (Luke
16:1–8). Jesus tells this story to a mixed gathering of
disciples and Pharisees. It is about a rich man who employed
a steward to manage his estates. After a time it was reported
to him that his steward was abusing his trust and squander-
ing his property.

He therefore sent for the man, demanded to see his accounts, and gave him notice of dismissal from his post. This put the steward in a quandary. What would he do for a living? He was not tough enough to take a laboring job, and he was too proud to beg. So he had to fall back on his wits. If he could build up a fund of good will around him by insuring that there would be a number of people who felt under an obligation to him, he could safeguard his future after his dismissal and at least satisfy himself that he would have a modest living. So he decided to fiddle the estate accounts before his employer could see them. Summoning the chief debtors first, presumably wholesale merchants, he got one man who owed the price of a thousand gallons of olive oil to alter the bill to read five hundred gallons. Another was owing for a thousand bushels of wheat. He was told to make out the bill for eight hundred bushels. So the steward went down the whole list of debtors in the same way. It meant that he was robbing his employer but, what was of more concern to him, he was creating a number of accomplices who, if this falsifying of the books were not discovered, would be in his power, keep their mouths shut, and maintain their benefactor in reasonable comfort.

We must assume that the plan miscarried and that the owner of the estate made sure that his money was safe, for the story ends with the employer commending his steward for his astuteness. He was a rascal, but his master applauds him for being a clever rascal. Jesus, in the words of our saying, associates himself with the employer not in commending the steward for his dishonesty, but in praising him for his ingenious plan which unfortunately for him did not come off. There is no question of our Lord's condoning the steward's unscrupulous behavior. Nor would the man's employer have had any words of praise for him if his scheme had worked. But he could not withhold admiration for the steward's intelligence and his determination to salvage what he could from the wreckage of his career. Jesus shares this admiration. By business standards the steward was displaying shrewdness and common sense in safeguarding his material future. Jesus is urging his other-worldly hearers—

disciples and Pharisees—to cultivate the same kind of single-mindedness in their pursuit of the spiritual life, a far more worthy cause than concern for their material welfare.

John Calvin went right to the heart of this parable when he wrote: "How stupid it is to want to interpret it in every detail! Christ simply meant that the children of this world are more diligent in their concern for their own fleeting interests than the sons of light for their eternal well-being." This is the point of the story which leads up to our Lord's comment. The steward is not being held up to us as a paragon of virtue—quite the contrary. He is recognized by his master and by Jesus as a crafty knave. But he is no fool. He is resourceful and he refuses to accept defeat, and these are good qualities in any man although in this case they are put to the wrong use.

We have all known or read of business tycoons who have sacrificed everything that most ordinary people value—home life, leisure, friends, and hobbies—in order to build up a fortune. Jesus' comment would mean that the church could do with more of this spirit, but directed into the channel of service of others and not for selfish ends. We are often told that as Christians we show up badly in zeal and enthusiasm compared with the energy and self-denial which Communists display in promoting their godless cause. As Christians we are committed to a service and a loyalty which far transcend allegiance to any earthly cause, and to a Master who demands all our skills and energy to play our part in the renewal of the life of society in his name. Jesus summons us from the pursuit of self-interest and self-enrichment to follow him along the way which he has marked out for us, and which he tells us is the way to life in all its fulness.

# 27

## DOING OUR DUTY

*When you have carried out all your orders,*
*you should say: "We are servants*
*and deserve no credit;*
*we have only done our duty."*

Luke 17:10

"DUTY" is a rather forbidding word. We remember from our schooldays that Wordsworth described duty as the "stern daughter of the Voice of God," and that at Trafalgar Nelson sent out the signal: "England expects that every man will do his duty." There is the suggestion in both that doing our duty is generally rather unpleasant. On his twenty-third birthday Milton wrote a sonnet in which he viewed life as being lived "as ever in my great Taskmaster's eye."

The parable (Luke 17:7–10) in which these words of Jesus' saying occur, likewise seems to stress the grimmer aspects of the service of God. It is a glimpse of a bygone state of society in a rural community which we are well rid of although doubtless there are still parts of the world where situations like this persist. The characters are a farmer and his slave, and there is no suggestion on the part of Jesus that their relationship was in any way unusual. He neither praises nor blames the attitude of the farmer but simply uses the illustration as one of the facts of peasant life. The slave comes in from the fields after a hard day's work. He might not unreasonably expect a meal. But the farmer, who has only one slave, expects him not only to plough and tend the cattle all day outside, but at the end of the day to cook the supper, wait at table, and wash up, before he gets anything to eat himself. For all this there is no word of thanks or sign of gratitude. The man has just done what he was told to do, and was expected to do as a matter of course. He has simply earned his keep.

Jesus now, in the words of our saying, draws a parallel between the relationship of the farmer and his slave, and the relationship between the Christian disciple and God. When you have obeyed all the commandments of God, he says, you deserve no credit. You have only done what is your duty. This picture of God as the all-demanding Taskmaster is much less attractive than the picture of God as the Father in the story of the Prodigal Son (Luke 15:11–32). Yet it is a useful corrective to much slushy sentimentalism, which tends to overlook the rigorous demands of God altogether. "Our picture of God," says Charles Coulson, "must resemble more the violence of a sunset painting by Turner than, as one of my friends once put it, a watery wash by a maiden aunt."

Elsewhere in Luke's Gospel (12:35–37) there is a glimpse of a different kind of relationship between a master and his slaves, or between God and his faithful servants, than that given in our present parable. Their faithfulness is rewarded by the master himself making them sit down to a meal and waiting on them at table. This is the way we prefer to think of God, as merciful and compassionate, loving us and caring for us. And of course this is true, but there is also the complementary truth about God which Jesus underlines in our present story. Nathan Soderblöm got the balance right when he said: "Only with God's good hand and strict bridle can the soul be helped to give its best." "God's good hand," yes, we can happily acknowledge that and all that it implies—lavishing on us the gift of life, bestowing blessing upon blessing, guiding and supporting us through all our difficulties, strengthening us by his grace on our journey. But "God's strict bridle," do we not also need that? As servants of God we need his discipline as well as his mercy.

If we take our Christian faith seriously, we have to recognize that the relationship between God and ourselves, between the Creator and his creatures, is one of God's absolute authority and our absolute dependence. This is the message that rings out loud and clear in the Bible, from the first chapter of Genesis onward. God owes us nothing: we owe God everything. Like the slave in the parable we can take no credit for any good we do, for it is God who gives us the power to do it. We have only done our duty and earned our keep. We deserve no thanks from God. If the farmer in the story can expect as his right the total commitment of his slave to his service, how much more right has God to expect the service of his creatures.

As servants of God there is an obligation laid upon us to serve our fellow men in the spirit of Christ's service, and in the light of his example. There is no point at which we can stand back and say: I have done enough. St. Paul who was tireless in his missionary activities understood Jesus' saying very well. "Even if I preach the gospel," he says, "I can claim no credit for it; I cannot help myself; it would be a misery to me not to preach" (I Cor. 9:16). And as we know, he did not content himself with merely preaching. There was no act of service which he considered beneath his dignity. He lived his life in the spirit of George Herbert's lovely hymn:

> *Teach me, my God and King,*
> *In all things Thee to see;*
> *And what I do in anything,*
> *To do it as for Thee!*
>
> *A servant with this clause*
> *Makes drudgery divine;*
> *Who sweeps a room, as for Thy laws,*
> *Makes that and the action fine.*

This hard saying of Jesus is a salutary corrective in our moods of self-pity. We feel that we are doing more than our share, in our jobs, in the home, in the work of the church. This point never comes, says Jesus, for you have only done your duty. It is also a cure for our pride, our feeling that in a variety of ways we are better Christians than our neighbors, more charitable, more sympathetic, more active in good causes. Not so, says Jesus, whatever you have done you have only done your duty. Yet if we take these apparently harsh words to heart, and live by them, we find that by the strange alchemy of God's providence his service turns out to be our perfect freedom.

# 28

## THE KINGDOM OF GOD

*In fact the Kingdom of God is among you.*

ONE OF THE DIFFICULTIES in reading the Bible is its special vocabulary. Words and phrases no longer in common use crop up frequently, and with the best will in the world modern translators cannot improve on the traditional language, and have to leave things as they stand. Such a phrase as "the kingdom of God" comes into this category. What generally happens is that we tend to be content with a vague idea of what it means, but in this saying of Jesus in Luke 17:21 we need to have more than just a vague idea. For if we look at the margin in the New English Bible we see that the words that follow "the kingdom of God" may be "is among you" or "is within you" or "is within your grasp" or "will suddenly be among you." These obviously do not mean the same thing.

"The kingdom of God" really means the sovereignty or kingly rule of God. The phrase is not found in these actual words in the Old Testament; but the idea was there from early times that the power of evil in the world would not last forever, and that one day God would confound his enemies, vindicate his chosen people Israel, and inaugurate a new age of peace and righteousness. By the time of Jesus, religiously minded people had come to the conclusion that the world had become so corrupt that nothing short of a cataclysmic end to the old order and the creation by God of a new heaven and a new earth would make it possible for the kingly rule or kingdom of God to begin. This was the point of the

Pharisees' question in Luke 17:20. They ask Jesus: "When will the kingdom of God come?" His reply is in effect that they are asking the wrong kind of question and he adds the difficult words of our saying: "In fact the kingdom of God is among you."

We have noted the variety of ways in which the rare Greek word *entos* may be translated. But the traditional (King James Version) translation "within you" led many readers of this passage off on a false scent. Even J. B. Phillips, who is usually right, follows the King James in his modern version and renders the saying of Jesus: "the kingdom of God is inside you." This suggests that the kingdom of God is some kind of spiritual element in each of us which, if it is cultivated, will in due course transform society. It puts the emphasis on man rather than on God. In the unaltered version of the nineteenth-century hymn "Rise Up, O Men of God," in verse 3 we used to sing: "Rise up, O men of God! The Church for you doth wait. Her strength unequal to her task; Rise up and make her great." But it is not men who can make the church great; it is the church that can make men great. So the hymn as now revised properly reads: "Rise up, O men of God! The Church for you doth wait. His strength shall make your spirit strong, Her service make you great." Jesus did not think of the kingdom of God as some utopian society which men would build by their own efforts with a little help from God. This would be in P. T. Forsyth's words: "A kingdom of man with God to serve in it, rather than a Kingdom of God with man to serve in it."

When we are in doubt in a matter of this kind it is often helpful to look at similar sayings of Jesus elsewhere in the Gospels. There is such a saying in this same Gospel of Luke. Jesus has just healed a dumb man and enabled him to speak. In the thought of the times the man had been possessed by a demon or devil, and Jesus' exorcism of this evil spirit had restored the man's speech. There were some present, however, who attributed the cure not to the power of God working through Jesus, but to the power of Satan. In his reply to this charge, which of course Jesus totally refutes, he says this: "If it is by the finger [i.e. the power] of God that I drive out the devils, then be sure the kingdom of God has already come among you" (Luke 11:20).

It is obvious from this that Jesus is not thinking of the kingdom of God as being in any way "inside" people. J. B. Phillips recognizes that in his translation of this verse: "If it is by the finger of God that I am expelling evil spirits, then the kingdom of God has swept over you here and now." Clearly Jesus is thinking of the kingdom of God as the kingly rule of God present in the world in a new way, associated with himself, and evidenced by the routing of evil in all its forms, including disease. The kingdom or rule of Satan over men's lives is crumbling and is being replaced by the kingdom or rule of God, ushered in by God's appointed Messiah.

Coming back, then, to our Lord's saying in Luke 17:21: "the kingdom of God is among you," we can find in it the key to Jesus' whole ministry. From his baptism onward our Lord regarded himself as God's agent, not only proclaiming that the new age had come, but embodying it in his own words and actions. Jesus was himself the Kingdom of God, as Origen said, summoning men to accept the sovereignty of God over their lives, teaching them in the Sermon on the Mount, in his parables, and elsewhere, the new way of life that God expected from those who would be citizens of his kingdom. His healing miracles were signs of the kingdom of God in action, restoring the broken in mind and body to health and sanity. His care and concern for the outcasts of society were living illustrations of the wideness of God's mercy, his forgiveness of sinners was absolution from God himself.

# 29

## BORN AGAIN

*Unless a man has been born over again*
*he cannot see the kingdom of God.*

John 3:3

MANY OF US are inclined to be suspicious of the term "born again." It tends to be used as a description of themselves by those who buttonhole complete strangers and ask them if they have been "saved." The implication is that no one can properly be called a Christian who has not experienced a conversion from unbelief to faith so sudden that it can be dated to the exact day and hour. That many have become Christians in this way throughout the history of the church is beyond question. The conversion of St. Paul is the classic example, where the arch-persecutor of the first Christians set out from Jerusalem determined to root out the Nazarene heresy, but on the road to Damascus Christ, as he says, took hold of him (Phil. 3:12; Acts 22:3–11).

To the matter-of-fact person—Christian or otherwise—who distrusts the emotional experience of the "born again" and argues that auto-suggestion or drugs can produce the same effect, these words of H. G. Wood are worth pondering: "There may have been a neurotic element in the make-up of Saul of Tarsus, John Bunyan and George Fox, and this may account for some features in the story of the conversion of each. But in all three examples, the man is re-made psychologically, morally and intellectually by his vision. This does not happen to the drug addict." But was this experience of the "born again" what our Lord was speaking of in the words of our saying in John 3:3?

The setting of the saying is a conversation between Jesus and Nicodemus, a leading Pharisee in Jerusalem, sympathetic to Jesus but too cautious to approach him openly. So he calls on him at night. We are given merely the gist of the conversation but it would seem that Nicodemus, impressed like many others by recent healing acts of Jesus, saw him as undoubtedly a "teacher sent by God" and wished to hear more from him. Nicodemus must at some point have asked the same question as was asked by the rich man in Mark 10:17: "What must I do to win eternal life?" for we are given Jesus' answer. In the Gospels, Matthew, Mark, and Luke generally use the phrase "kingdom of God" while John tends to speak of "eternal life," both terms meaning the same thing. However, whereas in Mark's Gospel the rich man asked about "winning eternal life" Nicodemus' question would seem to have been phrased in terms of the "kingdom of God," for in his reply Jesus says, "Unless a man has been born over again he cannot see the kingdom of God."

Once we have recognized that "winning eternal life" is the same as "seeing the kingdom of God" we may turn to Matthew's Gospel (18:3) and look at some words of Jesus on this same subject. He is teaching his disciples the necessity for humility and, taking a small child as a living illustration, Jesus says: "Unless you turn round and become like children you will never enter the kingdom of Heaven" (Matthew's gospel uses "kingdom of Heaven," meaning exactly the same as "kingdom of God"). Turning around and becoming like children, that is, casting away our pride and self-sufficiency and relying on God alone, in dependence and humility, is thus, according to Jesus, the only way to enter the kingdom of God, or the kingdom of Heaven, or to win eternal life.

It is clear therefore that when Jesus tells Nicodemus that a man must be "born again" before he can see, that is, experience or enter the kingdom of God, he means the same thing as "becoming like children." His words are thus applicable to ordinary people, and imply commitment of their whole life to God in obedience and trust, rather than demanding that all true Christians must experience the sudden conversion of the self-styled "twice-born." Yet although we may fight shy of the claims of the "twice-born," the Christian life is based on a rebirth, as Jesus makes plain in his words to Nicodemus. All of us are born into the world by natural processes, but the Christian life involves a second birth, which in Jesus' words means being born "from water and spirit" (John 3:5).

Christian baptism, implying a break with the past, and embarking on a new life under the control and in the power of God's Spirit, is of the essence of being "born again." Jesus likens the activity of the Spirit to the wind (John 3:8)—and in Greek the same word is used for wind and spirit. We know that the wind blows, we hear the sound of it, but we do not know where it comes from or where it is going. Similarly with the effect of the Spirit on a man's life. Having committed himself to God he is thenceforward under the control of God's Spirit, which is remaking his life, and raising it to a new dimension. Being born again, although it is the prerequisite of experiencing the rule of God over our lives, is only the beginning of the process.

Jeremiah asked the question that we all must ask: "Can the Nubian change his skin or the leopard its spots? And you? Can you do good, you who are schooled in evil?" (Jer. 13:23). We ask ourselves, How can a man become different from what he is, how can a cruel man become kind, how can a callous man become sensitive to other people's sufferings? The answer of both Old and New Testament is that he cannot, but God can do it for him. So Ezekiel assures us that God can take away our hearts of stone and give us hearts of flesh and put a new spirit within us (Ezek. 36:26). So the Psalmist calls on God who alone can do this: "Create a pure heart in me, O God, and give me a new and steadfast spirit" (Ps. 51:10). So Jesus answers Nicodemus in our saying, and so St. Paul spells it out for us in the magnificent eighth chapter of his letter to the Romans (Rom. 8:1–17).

# 30

## JEWS

*It is from the Jews that salvation comes.*

FREDERICK THE GREAT is said to have asked the Marquis d'Argens: "Can you give me one single irrefutable proof of God?" "Yes, your Majesty," was the reply, "the Jews." Alan Richardson has written: "Religious or secularised, the Jew remains a Jew—malgré lui a voluntary or involuntary witness to the truth that is symbolised in the story of God's Covenant with Abraham." The Chosen People, as a description of the Jews, has more often been used as a wry jest than as a tribute to a unique race. After four thousand years in which nation after nation in the ancient as well as in the modern world has sought to eliminate them, the Jews tenaciously retain their identity and at least some vestiges of their religion.

Christianity's debt to the Jews is immeasurable, which makes the past record of the church in relation to them all the more indefensible. Grudging respect for their business acumen, and their considerable contribution to literature and music has been overshadowed in popular thinking by the feeling that Shakespeare's Shylock was more than a caricature; and in the minds of religious people from the New Testament writers onward the fact that the Jewish church rejected Christ has proved an almost insuperable obstacle to a fair and balanced judgment on what we owe to the Jewish race. We are more likely to echo W. N. Ewer's memorable words: "How odd/ Of God/ To choose/ The Jews," than to subscribe to the verdict of Pope Pius XI that: "Spiritually we are all Semites."

For this hard saying of Jesus in John 4:22 is nothing

91

but the plain truth for all who call themselves Christians: "It is from the Jews that salvation comes." These words occur in the course of the fascinating story of the encounter between Jesus and the Samaritan woman at Jacob's well (John 4:1–30). The discussion involved the rival claims of the Samaritans and the Jews to have the true temple and the true faith. The Samaritans in Jesus' day, who occupied the territory between Judea and Galilee, regarded themselves as inheritors of the true religion of Moses and as descendants of the ten tribes of Israel. The feud between them and the Jerusalem Jews went back to the settlement of foreigners in their land by Assyria after the fall of the northern part of the divided kingdom of Israel in 721 B.C. (II Kings 17:24). There had been further trouble between the Jews and the Samaritans at the time of the Return from the Exile (Ezra 4; Neh. 6) as a result of which the Samaritans built their own temple on Mt. Gerizim, ignored the Temple at Jerusalem, and accepted as their Holy Scripture only the Pentateuch, the Law of Moses, discarding the later books of the Old Testament, including the Psalms and the Prophets.

Orthodox Jerusalem Jews dismissed the Samaritans as schismatics and had as little as possible to do with them. Jesus, however, on this occasion having asserted firmly that the worship of God does not depend on the place where he is worshiped—Gerizim or Jerusalem—but on the quality and nature of the worship, asserts equally firmly that the salvation of mankind depends on the knowledge of God contained in the Scriptures as a whole and not in the truncated version preferred by the Samaritans. The legacy of Israel in Jesus' view therefore is the total revelation of God's nature and purpose as enshrined in the Law, the Prophets, and the Writings, and it is from this in all its fulness that salvation comes. It was thus neither narrow nationalism nor blind patriotism that lay behind Jesus' words, nor a reflection of a sectarian dispute between two small religious groups in the ancient world, but a vital recognition of the supreme importance of the faith of Israel for the life of the world.

If we were asked to express Christianity's debt to the Jews we should probably begin by acknowledging that our

Lord and the apostles, not least St. Paul, were all Jewish. The church was founded by Jesus to be the new Israel, and it was Jews who were the first to carry the gospel to the pagan world. Later when Palestine was ravaged by the Romans and Jerusalem was sacked, the church became a predominantly Gentile institution, and its Jewish origins were conveniently ignored. For centuries bitterness, misunderstanding, and persecution marked the relationship between Christians and Jews. Indeed, it is only in very recent years that serious attempts have been made to repair the damage in a new spirit of tolerance and cooperation.

Christians are coming more and more to recognize that Christianity has never been a wholly new religion but is in fact a reformed type of Judaism. The faith of Jesus and his disciples was the faith of Old Testament psalmists and prophets, and our Lord's teaching is firmly anchored in the Law of Moses. When Jesus summed up all the commandments in the two great commandments, to love God and to love our neighbor, he took the words directly from the Old Testament (Deut. 6:5; Lev. 19:18; Mark 12:28–31); and St. Paul in making faith in God the heart of the gospel for Jews and Gentiles alike calls Abraham the father of us all (Rom. 4:16).

But of course Christians are not Jews and Jews are not Christians, and there is no point in closing our eyes to the difference. It is not merely a matter of circumcision or kosher food. Only strictly orthodox Jews meticulously observe their dietary regulations or keep separate sets of cooking utensils for themselves and their Gentile friends—or for that matter treat Sabbath observance as a fetish. The real issue is the status and uniqueness of Jesus. For Jews who share the Old Testament with Christians, the Messiah for whom psalmists and prophets hoped and prayed is still awaited. Jesus was at best the greatest of the prophets. No Jew would accept Jesus' words: "Anyone who has seen me has seen the Father" (John 14:9); the Cross is still for them a stumbling block as it was in St. Paul's day (I Cor. 1:23); and the Resurrection is a fantasy. Salvation does indeed come from the Jews, as Jesus said, but only by recognizing Jesus as their Savior and ours.

# 31

## LIFE AND DEATH

*Anyone who gives heed to what I say*
*and puts his trust in him who sent me*
*has hold of eternal life,*
*and does not come up for judgement,*
*but has already passed from death to life.*

John 5:24

IN THE APOSTLES' CREED we declare our belief in "the life everlasting." Some people find the thought of life "going on and on" unattractive, especially if they have been none too happy in the life they have had to live, through illness or misfortune. Most modern translations tend to use the word "eternal" instead, which is less open to misunderstanding. Jesus said: "I have come that men may have life, and may have it in all its fullness" (John 10:10). A full life, a life which is rich in experience of God, life lived on a higher plane, is a kind of life that everyone would surely wish to continue forever. This then is what Jesus promises, not a life that begins after death but a new kind of life that can begin here and now.

Some words of Baron von Hügel are worth reflecting on: "Only an eternal life already begun and truly known in part here, though fully to be achieved and completely to be understood hereafter, corresponds to the deepest longings of man's spirit as touched by the prevenient Spirit, God." In the words of our saying in John 5:24 Jesus lays down two conditions for knowing the beginning of eternal life in this imperfect world and with our unpromising background— obedience to his teaching and trust in God.

It is all too easy to speak of Christian obedience, but far from easy to put Jesus' teaching into practice. If we are honest with ourselves, we recognize how far short we come in approaching the standards that Christ has laid down, for example in the Sermon on the Mount. It is a demand for total unselfishness and generosity of spirit, and this is beyond the reach of anyone but a saint. Yet at the same time as we recognize our own shortcomings, we cannot but acknowledge that some ordinary men and women whom we have known in the course of our lives have come close to sainthood. Courageous in adversity, sympathetic with the problems and sufferings of others, charitable in their judgments, warm-hearted and compassionate, they have not only inspired us by their example, but strengthened our faith in God.

For clearly any man or woman who is trying to follow in Christ's footsteps must share to some extent Jesus' own attitude to God as Father. His sense of sonship, that intimate relationship to God strengthened by prayer and issuing in service, must be the foundation of any truly Christian living. And we have indeed, again in our own experience, often recognized in others the signs of God-centered lives. Their Christian obedience has not sprung from a frantic effort to comply with Jesus' teaching, but from a deep-seated trust and dependence on God. It shines through their actions, colors their outlook, and makes us feel that God is with us, too, as he so obviously is with them. These good souls, says Jesus, are already experiencing eternal life here and now, as they will know it more fully hereafter.

Let us look now at the second half of this saying of Jesus in John 5:24. What does he mean by claiming that such people do not "come up for judgement," and that they have "already passed from death to life?" Men have always been interested in the question of what happens after death. The brevity of man's life, even the allotted "threescore years and ten," but so often far less, was very much in the minds of the Old Testament writers. Yet it is only rarely that they look forward to anything beyond death other than the dismal prospect that faced Job in his black despair as he spoke of his impending departure to "a land of gloom, a land of gathering shadows, of deepening darkness, lit by no ray of light, dark upon dark" (Job 10:20–22).

The New Testament writers on the other hand were utterly convinced that the coming of Christ had changed all that. Death was no longer a voyage into the unknown but into the presence of Christ who had himself conquered death and now awaited his faithful people. Yet although for the New Testament writers nothing was more certain than that death is not the end of everything, they are wisely reticent on what exactly lies beyond it. They did not speculate and do not encourage us to do so either. They are content to affirm their faith in life after death, but they know that anything we say about an order of existence so different from our own can only be in terms of symbol and imagery. We may echo William Temple's words about the life beyond: "There is nothing in the world of which I feel so certain. I have no idea what it will be like, and I am glad that I have not, as I am sure it would be wrong."

Christian artists have let their imaginations run riot in depicting a Last Judgment at the end of time, with rewards and punishments handed out in accordance with our achievements or failures. The Fourth Gospel points us to a deeper interpretation of the mind of Jesus. Those who heed the teaching of Jesus, and put their trust in God, are judging themselves here and now by their response to Christ's words. They do not therefore come up for judgment at the end of time or even when they die. We have a choice here and now between following the way of life or the way of death. If we choose the way of life, the way of obedience to Christ and faith in God, we have already died to our past failures and are now alive in Christ, which is life eternal. The dissolution of our physical bodies, when that happens or how it happens, is a matter of no moment. St. Paul understood this well when he wrote to the Thessalonians: "God has not destined us to the terrors of judgement, but to the full attainment of salvation through our Lord Jesus Christ. He died for us so that we, awake or asleep [i.e. in life or in death], might live in company with him" (I Thess. 5:9–10).

# 32

## THE BREAD OF LIFE

*I am the bread of life. Whoever comes to me*
*shall never be hungry, and whoever believes in me*
*shall never be thirsty. . . .*
*Whoever eats my flesh*
*and drinks my blood dwells continually in me*
*and I dwell in him.*

*John 6:35, 56*

BEFORE LOOKING more closely at these words it is perhaps worth noting that they constitute the original "hard saying" (Revised Standard Version) in the sense that many of Jesus' disciples found it difficult to swallow, or, as the New English Bible puts it, they exclaimed: "This is more than we can stomach" (John 6:60). The saying is only one of several similar utterances of Jesus reported only in the Fourth Gospel, which many modern disciples also find difficult. In the first three Gospels Jesus usually describes himself as the Son of Man, but in this Gospel he makes claims on behalf of himself which appear to be much more far-reaching than the title Son of Man—which is sometimes just another way of saying "I," as when he says: "The Son of Man has nowhere to lay his head" (Matt. 8:20).

But in St. John's Gospel we find Jesus not only saying, I am the Bread of life, but also I am the Light of the world, I am the Door, I am the good Shepherd, I am the Resurrection and the Life, I am the Way, the Truth, and the Life, I am the true Vine. It has long been recognized that the Fourth Gospel differs in many respects from the other three Gospels, not least in its picture of Jesus. William Temple has well described it as the difference between a series of photographs of Jesus, which the first three Gospels give us, and a portrait of Jesus, which is what we get in the Fourth

Gospel. Here we are given not so much an exact verbatim record of Jesus' actual words, but rather the meaning and significance of what Jesus said, not least for the writer of the Gospel himself. The question of who wrote the Fourth Gospel has been much discussed, and there are many problems unsolved; but we shall not go far wrong if we think that it depends ultimately on John the son of Zebedee, one of the twelve disciples, who in his old age, after a lifetime of reflection and meditation on what Jesus had done and said, gives us this incomparable portrait of his Master, and brings us closer to the mind of Jesus than any other book in the New Testament.

The great discourse of Jesus, in which he calls himself the Bread of life, occupies most of chapter six of John's Gospel. The discourse is sparked by John's account of the Feeding of the Multitude, which appears in all four Gospels, and is best understood as a sacramental occasion. The crowd associated this with one of the best-remembered traditions of the Exodus, when in their flight from Egypt, under the leadership of Moses, the Israelites were sustained by what appeared to them to be a miraculous gift of bread from heaven. This was an edible exudation from tamarisk trees, so unfamiliar that they called it manna, meaning "What is it?" (Exod. 16). The Galilean crowd at once identify Jesus as the new Moses, but he turns their thoughts away from this, and from perishable food, to the spiritual nourishment which God gives, and which is the true bread from heaven.

Jesus then goes on in the words of our saying to claim that he himself is that bread, which communicates life to all who come to him, promising satisfaction of their spiritual needs, so that those who believe in him will no longer hunger and thirst for God's blessing and God's forgiveness. Isaiah had invited his countrymen to take part in a symbolic messianic banquet where water, bread, wine, and milk stand for the free gift of God's grace to those who hunger and thirst after righteousness, and are promised new life if they pay heed to the words which God speaks through his servants the prophets (Isa. 55:1–3). As the symbolic bread of life and water of life, Jesus thus claims to give life which is eternal to all who have faith in him.

These metaphors point forward to the climax of the discourse when the symbolic eating and drinking becomes mystical and sacramental. The eucharistic undertones which pervade this whole sixth chapter now become explicit: "Whoever eats my flesh and drinks my blood," says Jesus, "dwells continually in me and I dwell in him" (v. 56). These words enshrining the essence of the eucharistic liturgy can hardly have been spoken by Jesus as part of a sermon in the synagogue at Capernaum during his Galilean ministry and before the Last Supper had been celebrated, as would appear from verse 59. Once again, as in the story of Nicodemus, where Christian baptism is foreshadowed (John 3:5), the later faith and practice of the church in the Eucharist is assumed in the words attributed to Jesus here.

Gabriel Moran has said: "The Eucharist is the Church at her best." But one might almost say that the disputations about the Eucharist, about what it means and what it involves for the believing communicant, have shown the church at her worst. Perhaps Richard Hooker has been wiser than many ancient and modern theologians, who have sought to analyze and define precisely how the eucharistic bread and wine are related to the body and blood of Christ. "Let it therefore be sufficient for me," he says, "presenting myself at the Lord's Table, to know what I receive from him, without search or enquiry of the manner how Christ performeth his promises."

The hymn writers and the poets have always been better able to lead us to the heart of the Eucharist than the theologians. Christians over the centuries have been content to say with Horatius Bonar,

> *Here, O my Lord, I see thee face to face;*
> *Here would I touch and handle things unseen,*
> *Here grasp with firmer hand the eternal grace,*
> *And all my weariness upon thee lean.*

This is what has taken men and women in all ages, and of all shades of belief and all levels of churchmanship, humbly and expectantly again and again to this sacred mystery, where in faith union with Christ they have found that his words are no empty promise.

# 33

## "AND WAS MADE MAN"

*Anyone who has seen me has seen the Father.*

*John 14:9*

THESE WORDS OF JESUS have been described as "the most
staggering saying in literature." They must of course be
taken in association with the many other sayings in the
Fourth Gospel where Jesus speaks of himself and his
relationship to God, in particular his claims to Sonship in a
unique sense. But this saying goes farther than any of them.
In the case of anyone but Jesus a person calling himself the
Son of God would put himself in the same category, to quote
C. S. Lewis, as a man calling himself a poached egg.

According to public opinion polls, even in this age of
dwindling allegiance to the church most people claim to
believe in God. This could mean anything or almost
nothing—an Old Man in the sky, the Life Force, the Great
Mathematician, some kind of vague Power that controls
everything. But this is not the kind of God the New
Testament speaks of—or for that matter the Old Testament.
The psalmists and prophets of Israel had handed on as their
legacy belief in God as the Creator of the universe, the Lord of
history, who holds the destinies of men and of nations in his
hand, yet who is at the same time merciful and compassionate, tender and forgiving, hating evil, but always ready to
forgive the penitent sinner.

This was the faith in which Jesus and the disciples,
like all devout Jews, had been brought up. But one of these
disciples, Philip, wanted something more. Jesus, in his
conversations with them, had almost invariably referred to
God as "Father." Now in the great Farewell Discourse which

is the climax of the Fourth Gospel (John 14–16) Philip says: "Lord, show us the Father, and we ask no more" (John 14:8). It is as if he were saying: We believe in God as we have been taught to believe through the Scriptures, but you talk of him as Father. Make it plain to us that he *is* our Father. What is he like? That is all we want. Jesus' reply, which leads up to our saying, is patiently reproachful. "Have I been all this time with you, Philip, and you still do not know me? Anyone who has seen me has seen the Father."

St. Augustine in famous words said: "Thou hast made us for thyself, and the heart of man is restless until it finds its rest in thee." But how do we know God, how do we find him, how do we know what he is like? Jesus quite simply says: You have only to look at me! Studdert Kennedy wrote: "To attempt to worship a God without a name is to attempt the impossible. . . . Religion is falling in love with God; and it is impossible to fall in love with an abstract God, he must have a name. . . . The Christian faith says boldly to mankind, 'Come, let us introduce you to God. His name is Jesus, and he was a carpenter by trade.' " There is a delightful story of a small girl who was being put to bed and wanted her mother to stay with her. Her mother said: "Don't worry, dear, you'll be all right. The angels will be watching over you while you sleep." The child replied: "But, Mummy, I want a skin face." Jesus is God with a "skin face."

The central doctrine of the church is the Incarnation. In the Nicene Creed we confess our faith in "one Lord Jesus Christ, the only begotten Son of God . . . who for us men and for our salvation came down from heaven and was incarnate by the Holy Ghost of the Virgin Mary, and was made man." St. John's Gospel puts it succinctly: "The Word became flesh; he came to dwell among us" (John 1:14). As the words we use express our thoughts, so God's Word expresses his thoughts. In the Creation story in the first chapter of Genesis we are told that God brought the world into being with his words: "God said, let there be. . . ." The created world is the expression of God's thoughts. So when the prophets of Israel gave God's messages to his people, they prefaced their utterances with the words: "Thus saith the Lord." God communicates his mind and purpose through words, and in this sense the whole Bible may be called the Word of God. When we say then that in Jesus God's Word was made flesh, we mean that Jesus is the self-expression of God in a human life, God expressed in human terms. God, who is ultimately incomprehensible, becomes comprehensible in the life and work of Jesus.

This is a truth that is not easy to grasp, but Jesus himself helps us in the verses following our saying: "I am not myself the source of the words I speak to you: it is the Father who dwells in me doing his own work. Believe me when I say that I am in the Father and the Father in me; or else accept the evidence of the deeds themselves" (John 14:10–11). Most of us are neither mystics nor saints. Not for us the direct overwhelming vision of God which some have had in the past. Not for us the intuitive insight which recognizes in Jesus of Nazareth "Very God of Very God." What we can, however, recognize is the power and presence of God in Christ's acts of healing and compassion, mending broken lives, straightening out twisted natures, giving new purpose to aimless drifters, turning despair to hope. The united testimony of harassed and troubled men and women down the ages is that "Jesus saves," saves us from our frustrations and failures, from self and sin, from disillusionment and doubt. If we "accept the evidence of the deeds themselves" as Jesus said, we are bound to acknowledge that he who can do these things must himself be God.

In the sacred mystery of the Eucharist we know that this is true, and echo Doubting Thomas's confession: "My Lord and my God" (John 20:28). We can say then with John Betjeman:

> No love that in a family dwells, no carolling in frosty air,
> Nor all the steeple-shaking bells can with this single Truth
>     compare—
> That God was Man in Palestine, and lives today in Bread and
>     Wine.

# 34

## CHRIST THE CONQUEROR

*I have conquered the world.*

John 16:33

THE FOURTH-CENTURY ROMAN EMPEROR JULIAN, generally known as Julian the Apostate since he sought to revive paganism soon after Christianity had been established as the state religion, is said to have died of a wound inflicted by one of his Christian soldiers. His last words were the wry comment: "Thou hast conquered, O Galilean." A. C. Swinburne, the Victorian poet, who also had no love for Christianity and thought of it as a blight which had brought doom and misery upon the carefree innocence of the pagan world, likewise spoke of Christ as a conqueror: "Thou hast conquered, O pale Galilean; the world has grown grey from thy breath."

Although many of our best-known hymns use the language of battle, such as "Onward Christian Soldiers," "Soldiers of Christ Arise, and Put Your Armour On," "The Son of God Goes Forth to War," no one has ever seriously thought of words like these as being anything other than metaphors. Napoleon certainly had no doubt about the nature of Christian warfare when he said: "Alexander, Caesar, Charlemagne and I have founded empires. But on what did we rest the creations of our genius? Upon force. Jesus Christ founded his empire upon love; and at this hour millions of men would die for him."

Yet the words of Jesus in this saying in John 16:33 are at first sight surprising, coming from one who is generally thought of as Christ the Prince of Peace rather than

103

as Christ the Conqueror. But what is even more surprising is the situation in which Jesus made this astonishing claim. It was the night before the Crucifixion, and Jesus, as the Fourth Gospel tells us, "knew that his hour had come" (13:1) and that he was about to be betrayed by one of his closest followers. He had in the action-sermon of washing his disciples' feet taught them the lesson of service to one another, and in the great discourse that followed had spoken of his love for them in laying down his life for them (15:13). Judas Iscariot had left the group bent on his fateful mission, Peter's denial of his Master was close at hand, and Jesus knew that the others would also forsake him. It was in this hour of desolation that he uttered the extraordinary cry of triumph in our saying: "Courage! The victory is mine; I have conquered the world." With these his last recorded words of teaching before his arrest in Gethsemane, he moved forward to his death not as to defeat but as to victory.

Carlyle was moved to tears by Jesus' words here which have been described as the most gallant in all literature. Everything that Jesus had tried to do had failed. He had sought to awaken his countrymen to their need for repentance, and had urged them to commit their lives to God. Most of them preferred to stay as they were. His small band of picked followers, over whose training he had spent so much time and effort, were now in his hour of crisis about to fail him. The malevolence of the religious authorities was massing to destroy him. The physical suffering of death by crucifixion was known in all its horror to every Jew who passed along the roads, with their wayside crosses burdened with the bodies of rebels against Roman rule. Of all this Jesus was well aware. When in Gethsemane, as Mark's Gospel tells us, Jesus spoke of his heart being ready to break with grief, and when he prayed that he might be spared this impending agony, there was little to suggest a victor who had conquered anything, let alone the world.

But let us look at the words that precede our saying in verses 31–33. Jesus sees himself being deserted by his friends, leaving him alone. Yet he will not be alone, for the Father is with him, now and always. This is the secret of his

strength and his courage. He who had never had outward
peace promises his followers peace in him. They will have
trouble in the world but let them take heart. Their Master
who has triumphed over all the afflictions that the world can
bring—opposition, distrust, hatred—will share his inward
peace with them and enable them to defeat all the evils that
will come upon them. They will conquer the world as he
himself has done.

So indeed it has proved to be in the experience of the
church through the centuries. The Christian lives in two
spheres. He is in the world with all its disappointments and
heartaches, its tensions and strife. But he is also in Christ, in
communion with him who has himself known the worst that
the world can do to us, and who has been victorious. The
peace that Christ gives his followers is not freedom from
anxiety, from worry, from misfortune, and from disaster, but
peace in the midst of conflict, a spirit in harmony with Christ
the Victor. "Every child of God is victor over the godless
world," says the first epistle of John. "The victory that
defeats the world is our faith, for who is victor over the world
but he who believes that Jesus is the Son of God?" (I John
5:4–5).

"We are more than conquerors through him who
loved us," cries St. Paul in that great outburst in his letter to
the Romans. "What can separate us from the love of Christ?
Can affliction or hardship? Can persecution, hunger, naked-
ness, peril, or the sword? 'We are being done to death for thy
sake all day long,' as Scripture says; 'we have been treated like
sheep for slaughter'—and yet, in spite of all, overwhelming
victory is ours through him who loved us. For I am convinced
that there is nothing in death or life, in the realm of spirits or
superhuman powers, in the world as it is or the world as it
shall be, in the forces of the universe, in heights or
depths—nothing in all creation that can separate us from the
love of God in Christ Jesus our Lord" (Rom. 8:35–39).